COURTLANDT CANBY   VOL. 2 | # a history of ships and seafaring

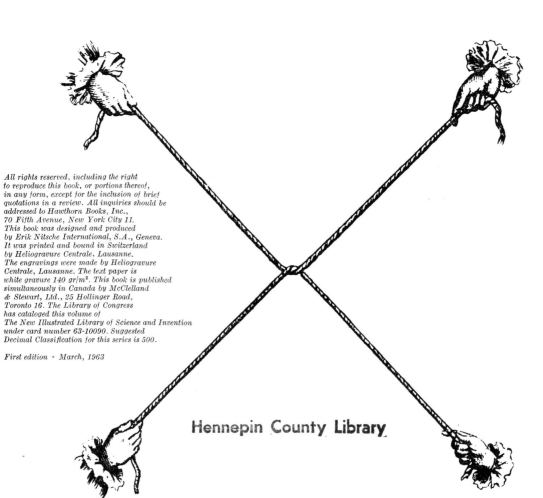

contents

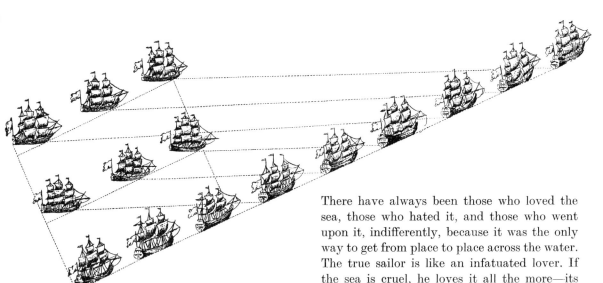

There have always been those who loved the sea, those who hated it, and those who went upon it, indifferently, because it was the only way to get from place to place across the water. The true sailor is like an infatuated lover. If the sea is cruel, he loves it all the more—its dangerous moods, its treachery, the struggle to master it. Dr. Johnson, who was no sailor, once said, "When men come to like a sea-life, they are not fit to live on land."

The true sailor has always been a gambler. His bones, and the bones of his ships, and the remains of the cargoes for which he gambled and lost, strew the floors of the world's oceans, providing a rich harvest for modern-day archaeologists. In the words of Shakespeare:

Methought I saw a thousand fearful wrecks,
Ten thousand men, that fishes gnawed upon;
Wedges of gold, great anchors, heaps of pearl,
Inestimable stones, unvalued jewels,
All scattered in the bottom of the sea.

The true sailor is also an adventurer at heart. Men of his breed, as Hakluyt wrote, have always been "full of activity, stirrers abroad, and searchers of the remote parts of the world." These men have been making history with their ships since the first adventurous mariner mounted a log and set out across a river for the other shore. For from the beginning of history until the advent of the ocean-spanning airplane (which was just the other day), the ship was the only way to get from continent to continent, from country to country, and often from place to place within a country, along the shoreline or up and down the rivers.

The ship carried trading goods, ideas, habits, wealth, tools, words, and people from nation to nation; it carried explorers and conquerors to new lands and to old; it was the chief agency in the spread of human civilization around the world. Thus the history of the ship is intimately tied in with the long history of mankind.

If the sailor and his ship made history, so did the landlubber in his own, landlocked way. Safe on the solid shore, he found it hard to understand why anyone should want to risk his life on the ocean. In Roman times Lucretius wrote, "How pleasant it is, when a gale of wind is blowing, to stand on the shore and watch the other fellow, out there, in trouble." Only once in the history of the sea has the landlubber interfered in matters maritime, and that was when he invented the steamboat in the eighteenth century. Even then he approached his invention as a mechanic would, being more interested in its engine than in its hull. Eventually the steamboat grew up, went out to sea, and was taken over by the sailor, who endowed it, as he had the sailing ship, with the special language, the romance, the *esprit de corps* typical of his calling. And in his hands the steamboat, in turn, began to make history.

But it was the sailing ship that dominated most of human history. Since it was not an invention, like the steamboat, but a slow development, there is a remarkable continuity in its story. Indeed in fundamentals the ship and seafaring changed very little for thousands of years, and in trade, exploration, and war, the principal functions of the ship in history, there were remarkable parallels between one period and another. The Sea Peoples of the first millennium B.C., like the Vikings of 2,000 years later, were pirates, superb seamen, who descended upon foreign lands first to burn and pillage, then to settle and enrich the growth of civilization. The Greeks and Phoenicians explored westward in the Mediterranean and out into the Atlantic just as (again 2,000 years later) the Portuguese, Spanish, Dutch, French, and English opened up a new world even further to the west. Rome's domination of the Mediterranean, a period of rich and peaceful trade, was preceded by a period of national rivalries and naval warfare under the successors of Alexander. So, too, was the Pax Britannica of the nineteenth century preceded by a long series of national rivalries on the sea. If these parallels illustrate anything, they emphasize the continuity and conservatism of seafaring history.

But conversely, they serve to emphasize another point: the changing nature of history in recent times. Over the last 300 years, with the advent of the industrial revolution and the development of the steamboat, the automobile, and the airplane, history has begun to run faster, and in new and different channels. Today it is no longer safe to trust the old parallels; we are entering a new phase of the world's history; we are losing touch with our own past. And the future of seafaring and of the ship has become as nebulous as everything else. Yet perhaps for a time we can still say, with the Psalmist, "They that go down to the sea in ships . . . these see the works of the Lord, and his wonders in the deep."

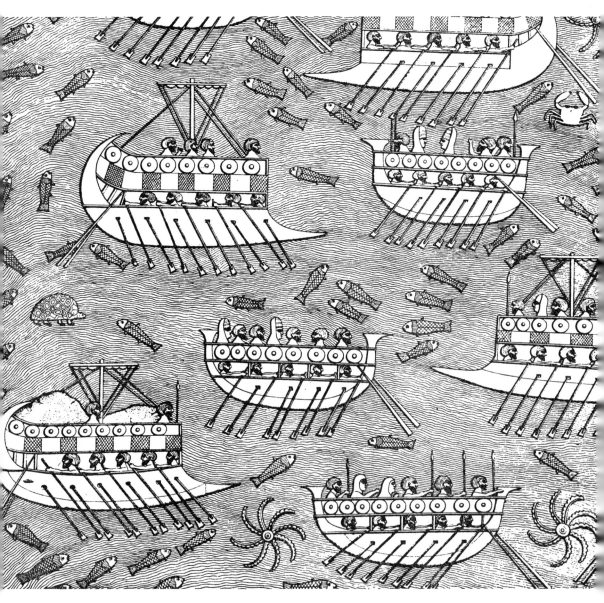

*1   The Assyrian fleet of King Sennacherib navigates
the waters near the Persian Gulf. War galleys are
beaked, transports are rounded.*

– *C*

"And God said, Let the waters under the heaven be gathered together unto one place, and let the dry land appear."

Man was cradled on the dry land, it was his birthplace. But the waters—the rivers and oceans—first nurtured that fragile plant, his civilization, and eventually helped to carry it around the world. Man both feared and loved the waters with a timeless fascination. With their floods, storms, and drownings they were a terror, and yet also a challenge. It took many thousands of years before man learned to use the rivers and the oceans to his advantage.

His civilization first appeared in the ancient valleys of the Nile, the Indus, and Mesopotamia, a mere five thousand years ago. The rivers in these valleys provided man not only with a wealth of water for his crops and an abundance of fish, but also with a safe and easy path up and down the land for that interchange of ideas, artifacts and people which promoted the growth of civilization. And since all these rivers led to the sea, man was soon tempted to venture out into the dangerous oceans in search of wealth in other lands. He took his civilization along with him.

But first there had to be vessels to carry him. A floating log or a bundle of reeds will support a man but cannot be called a boat. When the log was hollowed out, or was tied to others to make a raft, and the reeds were fastened together at each end, the boat appeared. The ship, however, had to wait for those technological advances—the plank construction, the oars and rudder, the mast and sail—that took place in Egypt and Mesopotamia at the dawn of civilization, probably during the fourth millennium B.C. At first the ship stayed safely within the rivers. Indeed the ships of Egypt, made of bundled papyrus or blocks of acacia wood or sycamore, had no keels and never became very seaworthy. But in time the Nile developed a bustling traffic ranging from tiny rowboats to royal yachts and immense barges for carrying the heavy obelisks.

Soon ships were venturing timidly into the seas in search of trade. Treeless Egypt, prizing the cedar wood from Syria, very early worked up an exchange of goods with Phoenician Byblos. Egyptians sailed, too, down the Red Sea to lower Africa in search of incense, myrrh and frankincense. About 2000 B.C. a wide canal was cut from the Red Sea to the Nile to facilitate this trade, and 500 years later Egypt's great queen, Hatshepsut, mounted a state expedition to Punt (perhaps Somaliland) that returned with rare woods and metals, cattle, apes and monkeys, natives, and even "a southern panther alive, captured for Her Majesty." From Mesopotamia, too, ships worked down the Persian Gulf in search of copper, precious stones, ivory and rare woods. There may even have been some trade with the great but short-lived Indus civilization.

Egypt's peak of power was reached in the New Kingdom, when it dominated the eastern Mediterranean, commanding chariots from Syria, cattle from Asia Minor, foods and copper from Cyprus, fabrics from Syria, and incense and ivory from Punt. During this period Egypt's powerful pharaoh, Thutmose III (1490-1436 B.C.) led 18 military campaigns into Syria, transporting his armies in ships.

But his keel-less transports and warships were still essentially river craft, and much of Egypt's commerce in this golden period was carried in foreign bottoms.

Crete was the first real seapower of the Mediterranean. Ruled by their fabulous King Minos from his palace at Knossos, the Cretans were called by the Egyptians the "people of the isles in the middle of the sea." They sailed, as befitted an island people, in sturdy, ocean-going ships, built with keels and ribs, and they traded widely from Sicily to Syria, leaving their distinctive pottery behind them and importing a wealth of luxuries for their labyrinthine palaces and well-built towns. They were a gay and pleasure-loving people, whose civilization in time spread to the mainland of Greece, bringing power and wealth to the vigorous, warlike Greeks of Mycenae and Pylos and other city states celebrated by Homer. Then about 1450 B.C., in a strange reversal, the Greeks of the mainland turned upon their masters and conquered them. Henceforth, and for several hundred years, Greeks and Cretans were one. Under mainland leadership the old trade was carried on and extended and the strengthened civilization of both Greeks and Cretans came to a peak of luxury and power.

Then it began to decline. Impelled by obscure tribal movements in the uncivilized north, bands of raiders began to descend upon the Mediterranean by sea and by land, cutting the vital trade routes upon which the Mycenaeans depended for their wealth and food. The overpopulated cities, falling upon hard times, turned against each other. Many of their inhabitants emigrated to other lands, or took

2 The earliest Egyptian boats were bundles of papyrus or reeds.
3 A small Egyptian grain ship.
4 In Mesopotamia inflated skins, as in this Assyrian relief, were used from earliest times.

to piracy with the raiders, known as the Sea Peoples. A final incursion of illiterate Dorian Greeks from the mountains gave the death blow to the Mycenaean civilization. Some scholars believe that the Trojan War was a last desperate effort by the harassed Mycenaeans to free the grain route to the Black Sea, closed to them by the power of Troy. Others see in the myth of Jason and the Golden Fleece an organized attempt, in a disturbed period, to seek out new sources of wealth to the north. Homer's *Odyssey* is filled with stories of sea raiders and piracy.

In a few centuries the long-nurtured civilization of the Bronze Age peoples of the eastern Mediterranean had been swept away. For this time of troubles was the watershed between the bronze and iron ages, and its ravages extended even to Egypt. "Lo, the northern countries . . . are restless in their limbs; they infest the ways of the harbormouths," wrote a scribe of Ramses III. Moving south by oxcart and in swift raiding ships, and their ranks swelled by dispossessed Greeks and others, the Sea Peoples looted and burned coastal cities throughout Greece, Syria, and Palestine, much like the Vikings of a later age. Several times the raiders attacked Egypt by land and by sea, but were finally repulsed by Ramses III in a great sea battle in 1190 B.C. Some were turned aside to Palestine, where they settled and became known as the Philistines.

After the fall of Mycenae, the Phoenicians were well prepared to take over command of the seas. Heirs of the Biblical Canaanites, they occupied a string of ports—Tyre, Sidon, and Byblos among them—that tapped the trade

2

3

4

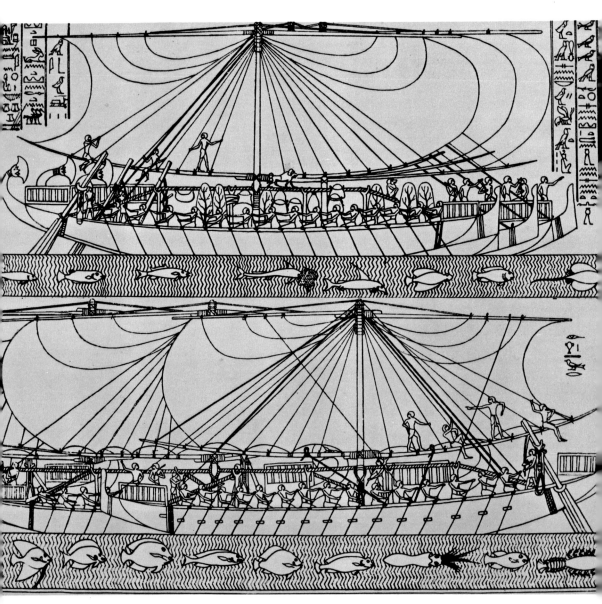

5 Ships of Queen Hatshepsut's trading
expedition to Punt carrying rare trees,
apes, and other exotic items on the return
journey to Egypt. Queen Hatshepsut, of
Egypt's New Kingdom, was one of the first
great women of history.

of the interior. Their sturdy ships were built of cedar of Lebanon, which they had long supplied to Egypt. Their cedars, too, went into Solomon's temple at Jerusalem, built about 970 B.C. Canny merchants, hardheaded, cruel and secretive, the Phoenicians were the middlemen of the Mediterranean, carrying the goods and ideas of civilization, like pollen on bees, from one country to another. "Thither came Phoenicians," sang Homer in his *Odyssey*, "men famed for their ships, greedy knaves, bringing countless trinkets in their black ship." Among the trinkets they brought to Greece was the first alphabet, which they had developed as an aid in their business. Another of their trade specialties was the "royal purple" cloth, dyed from the murex sea snail.

Venturing ever further westward—to Malta, Sicily, Sardinia, North Africa, and Spain—the Phoenicians brought back silver, lead, and iron. They may perhaps have even reached Britain in search of tin, and there is some evidence that Phoenician sailors, serving Pharaoh Necho, circumnavigated Africa from east to west around 600 B.C. About 100 years later Hanno of Carthage actually led an expedition along the west coast of Africa, planted several colonies, and returned with the skins of what must have been chimpanzees. As they explored, the Phoenicians planted trading stations, some of which became colonies— Cadiz in Spain, Utica, and Carthage in North Africa. Carthage, founded by Tyre, became in turn a great city, and by 700 B.C. had established its own colonies in Sicily, Sardinia, Malta, the Balearic Islands, and along the Mediterranean coast of Spain.

Around 800 B.C. the city states of Greece, emerging from their dark ages, began to plant their own colonies. Between 750 and 550 B.C., impelled by overpopulation at home as well as by trade, they founded some 250 outposts, from Byzantium to Marseilles. Wanderers at heart, the Greeks moved in organized groups, a part or sometimes the whole of a city embarking under a leader, or "oecist," for their new home. The Black Sea was ringed by colonies planted by Miletus. Corinth founded Syracuse in Sicily, and with other colonizing cities dotted the coasts of Sicily and southern Italy with outposts of Greek civilization. But north of Naples, they were stopped by the vigorous Etruscans, who dominated most of Italy before the Romans. Leagued with the Carthaginians, the Etruscans held the balance of power against the Greek colonies in the western seas.

Unlike the other Greeks, the Phocaeans of Asia Minor pushed westward in flotillas of warships rather than in merchantmen, reaching the Atlantic coast of Spain, hitherto a Phoenician preserve, and settling colonies, including Marseilles, along the Mediterranean coasts of France and Spain. Several times they met the Carthaginians in pitched battles at sea, leading the latter eventually to close the straits of Gibraltar to their competitors. In the fourth century, however, one great explorer, Pytheas of Marseilles, sneaked through the straits and sailed northward, rounding England and reaching the estuary of the Elbe and possibly even Scandinavia.

By the sixth century B.C. the period of colonization had waned, leaving the Mediter-

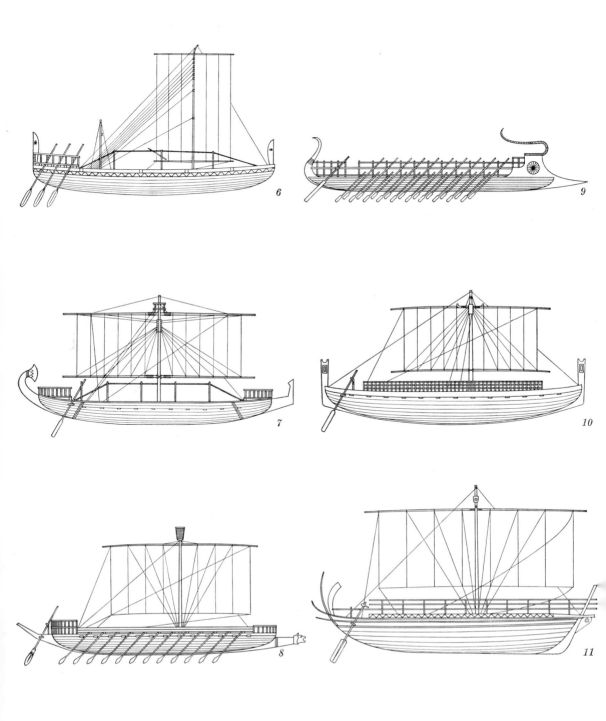

6

9

7

10

8

11

6 *Egyptian Nile ship, before 2000 B.C.*
7 *Sea-going Egyptian ship of c. 1500 B.C. used in Queen Hatshepsut's expedition to Punt. About 80 feet long.*
8 *Ramses III employed warships of this type in battles against the Sea Peoples.*
9 *Early Greek warship, about 1000 B.C.*
10 *Very early Greek merchantman.*
11 *Phoenician trading ship, c. 700 B.C.*
12 *Phoenician galley, an early bireme.*
13 *Small coastal Phoenician trading ship.*
14 *Elegant Greek bireme, about 500 B.C.*
15 *Greek trireme, with bronze-sheathed ram, was used by both sides at the Battle of Salamis (480 B.C.)*
16 *Roman galley, with fighting tower.*
17 *Roman merchantman. Some were 180 feet long, carried 600 or 700 passengers.*

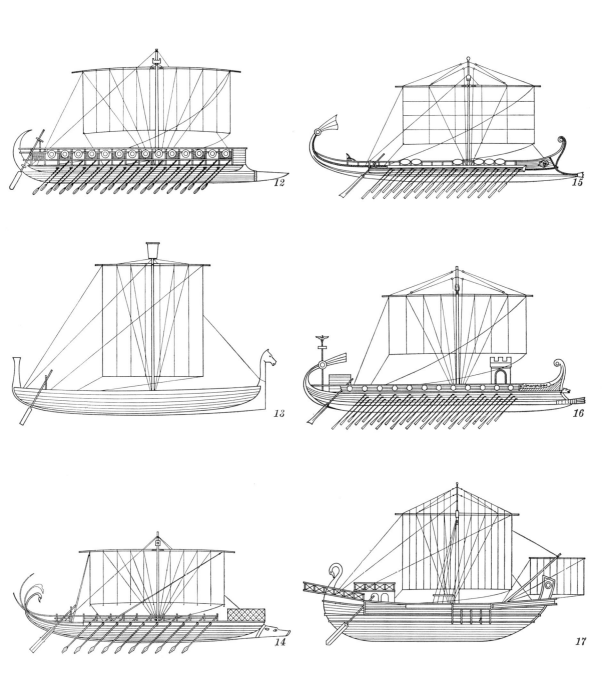

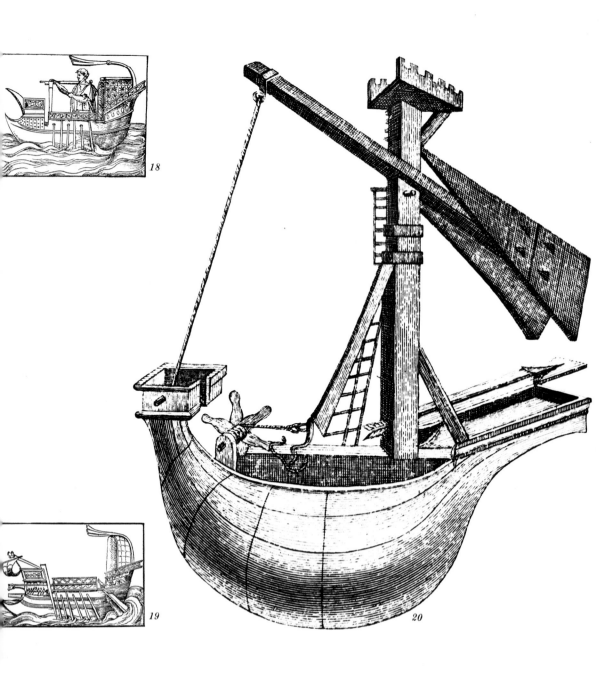

18 A 16th century conception
of a Roman bireme, which
differed little, except in size
and refinements, from the
original Greek model.
19 Another Roman bireme.
20 An 18th century view of a
Roman catapult warship.
From Hellenistic times onward
Greek and Roman warships
grew larger and were armed
with heavy catapults as well
as bowmen and spearmen.
21 Athenian galleys in a race,
as painted by Nicosthenes.

18

19

20

ranean webbed with busy trade routes. Big-bellied merchantmen, moving slowly under a single square sail, carried wine, oil, grain and trading goods from city to city, while fleets of fast warships kept pirates and rivals from the trading routes. These galleys were a far cry from the light, undecked raiders of the Mycenaeans. Equipped with a fighting deck and a powerful, bronze-sheathed ram at the prow, they depended upon the strength and precision of their many oarsmen to give the shattering blow that would sink an enemy. In battle the mainsail was left on shore, for the oar was king. The Phocaean galleys were fifty-oared penteconters. The later, two-banked galley, and finally the famous trireme, with a third bank of oars working from an outrigger, gave more power in a shorter, stronger hull. "One may imagine the noise of this great fleet getting away under oars all together," wrote Arrian of the fleet of Alexander the Great, "it was like nothing ever heard before, what with the coxswains calling the *in. .out, in. .out* for every stroke and the rowers' triumphant cries as, like one man, they flung themselves upon the swirling water."

Triremes fought on both sides at Salamis in 480 B.C. The armies of Xerxes, the Persian, swarming into Greece, had captured Athens, and his fleet, made up of ships from the Levant, Egypt, and Asia Minor, was ready for the kill. The great Athenian commander, Themistocles, relying upon the "wooden walls" of the oracle, lured the huge enemy fleet into the narrow waters of the Bay of Salamis, and with half its numbers, there reduced it to a shambles. The Persians were forced to withdraw.

Seapower had won a victory for the West. And it had won for Athens a century of supremacy on the eastern seas. The Athenian navy, some 400 strong, was the finest known, while Piraeus, the port of Athens, became a busy center for trade throughout the Mediterranean. But the strength of Athens, and of its navy, was gradually drained away in that exhausting, 27-year contest with Sparta known as the Peloponnesian War. Her enemies, too, learned to buttress their ships against the Athenian ram, while new types of ships appeared that reduced the importance of the trireme. The disastrous attempt to capture Syracuse in 415 B.C. cost Athens 200 ships and 50,000 men. The naval power of Athens was ended by Alexander the Great's successors in 322 B.C.

Like Xerxes, Alexander had picked up a fleet from the Greeks of Asia Minor and the Phoenicians as he swept eastward on his conquests. When Alexander died of a fever in Babylon in 323 B.C. he left behind him an area dominated by the Greeks which stretched from India to Spain. In its cultural unity, its opulence, its pursuit of bigness, the Hellenistic Age was a preview of the Roman Empire. Cargo ships, growing heavier in tonnage, crisscrossed the Mediterranean from end to end. Warships, too, grew larger and more specialized as Alexander's generals, dominating different parts of his empire, began a "battleship race" which reminds one of that which preceded World War I. Some 80 years before, Dionysius of Syracuse had invented the quadrireme and quinquereme (not, most scholars agree, four- and five-banked galleys but four or five men on each oar). Antigonus of Greece and his

21

navalminded son, Demetrius, began to construct even larger galleys, in the shipyards of Phoenicia, all the way up to a huge "sixteen." The Ptolemies of Egypt countered with bigger ships, including two immense "thirties." The frequent sea battles between these antagonists were like those of modern times, with stately "battleships," armed with heavy catapults, leading a balanced force of smaller "cruisers," and still lighter types like the trireme. Late in the third century Ptolemy IV climaxed the naval race with a mammoth "forty" with 4,000 rowers (probably on three banks of oars). Over 400 feet long and 50 feet wide, it was the size of a small steamer and was obviously built for display, not combat.

Far to the west the expanding Roman state was going through its period of trial. The Romans, a race of landlubbers, inevitably came up against the Carthaginians on the sea as they took over the Greek cities of southern Italy, and when the First Punic War broke out in 264 B.C. they had to build up a navy from scratch. But the Romans were a dogged people and 23 years later they ended the war with one of the finest navies afloat. The corvus, a movable, spiked gangplank which allowed the tough Roman legionnaires to board the enemy, was decisive in the early years. The bitter Second Punic War was a land war, because the Romans still held control of the seas, forcing Hannibal to invade Italy with his famous elephants. From it the Romans emerged as a seapower to be reckoned with.

In the meantime in the east the descendants of Antigonus and of Ptolemy had exhausted themselves in fruitless rivalry. The two great ports of the day were Alexandria in Egypt, with its fine harbor and great Pharos, or lighthouse, and the banking and commercial center of Rhodes, which held the balance between the two rivals. When Rhodes called on Rome for help in 201 B.C. a process of gradual infiltration began which in 170 years was to make the Mediterranean a Roman lake. Preferring to use the ships of her allies, Rome fought several wars with the Greek kings and increasingly drew the rich trade of the East toward her own voracious capital. In 67 B.C. Pompey cleaned out the pirates from the Mediterranean in a brilliant three-month's operation. The naval battle of Actium 36 years later (when Mark Antony and Cleopatra fled ignominiously before Augustus) brought an end to the bitter Roman civil wars. For the first time in history the Mediterranean had come under unified control.

Augustus set up a first-class navy, manned by seasoned Greek, Phoenician, and Egyptian sailors (none of them slaves), which policed the Roman seas from the English Channel to the Black Sea. Commerce flourished as never before, most of it funneling into Rome through her artificial port at Ostia, built after 42 A.D. Rome's merchants sailed around India to trade with Malaya, Sumatra, and Java, and even reached the borders of China. Great grain ships plied between Alexandria and Rome, some 180 feet long and capable of carrying 1,300 tons of cargo—and passengers, too, like the captive St. Paul. For some 400 years Rome's seapower ruled the oceans. Its like would not be seen again for well over a thousand years.

22 *River traffic on the flooded Nile in Roman times, including a two-banked galley, most likely a Liburnian or light warship attached to the fleet stationed at Alexandria in Egypt.*

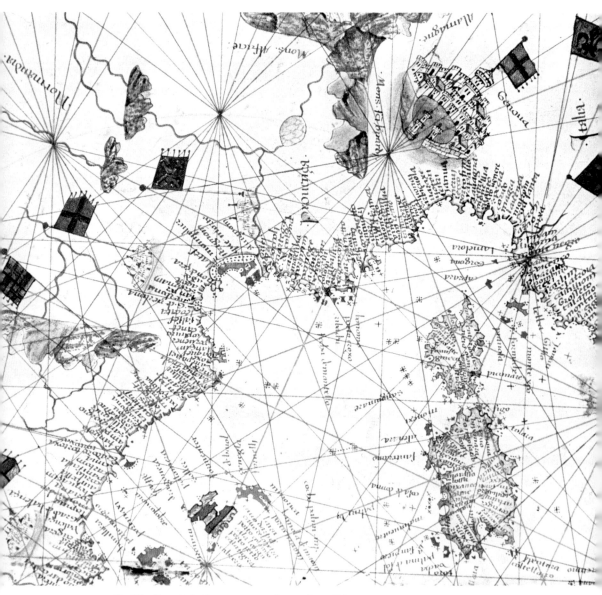

23 *The French-Italian coast near Genoa, in a 15th century map. For thousands of years seafaring history centered around the Mediterranean, until the rise of the northern nations and the exploration of the New World and the Orient made its scope world-wide.*

Although seafaring, like everything else, first developed in and around the Mediterranean, it was not long before men had taken to the waters in other parts of the world. Wherever there was a puddle, a river, a lake, or the shores of a sea, the more adventurous souls would take off, in some kind of boat or ship, in search of new horizons.

The seafaring impulse sometimes came from the Mediterranean. Sometimes it would be a new idea, springing from local needs. The Polynesians, for instance, were driven from the Asian mainland, perhaps in the third century B.C., and began moving eastward across the Pacific from island to island, peopling each one and then moving on to the next, until roughly a thousand years later their migrations had taken them as far as the central Pacific. They journeyed in great double canoes, propelled by a sail and 50 or more paddlers, with a platform at the center for the women, children, animals, plants, and supplies. As many as 300 canoes would venture out together, covering a vast front so that there would be less chance of missing their destination. Sometimes, as between the Marquesas and Hawaii, they would sail for as far as 21,300 miles without a landfall.

Back on the China coast the junk, built to sail with the monsoons, developed very early and changed little over thousands of years. The largest were floating emporiums, capable of carrying hundreds of people, with as many as four masts and sails. "They have a single deck," Marco Polo reported in 1298, "and under this the space is divided into sixty small cabins . . . each furnished as a small living quarters for a merchant." Though clumsy

SVH

24

25

26

sailers, the junks had watertight compartments, the stern rudder, and a primitive form of compass long before the European ships. And the Chinese were not afraid of the sea. In 1281 two huge fleets, one Chinese, one Korean, carried 150,000 Mongols across the sea to Japan for an attempted invasion.

The Arabs acted as middlemen between the Far East and the West for thousands of years. In Hellenistic times they shared the oriental trade with Indian merchants, and in the early Middle Ages negotiated the monsoons to China and back in palatial merchant ships copied from the Chinese junk. They may have borrowed the compass, too, from China and passed it on to Europe. In the eighth century A.D. the Arab dominions stretched from India to Spain. Baghdad, the Abbasid capital, was a huge and busy port. Its miles of docks received silk and musk from China, spices and dyes from India, rubies, furs, honey, and slaves from Central Asia, Russia, and Scandinavia, and ivory from West Africa. In the Mediterranean the Arabs (like the Persians and the Romans before them) had acquired ships and sailors from the ancient ports of Egypt and the Levant. By the ninth century they had taken Cyprus, Crete, and Sicily and were threatening Constantinople. East faced West across the inland sea.

During their initial expansion the Arabs had mounted a savage, five-year attack upon Constantinople, capital of the Eastern Roman Empire, which had been beaten off by the Byzantine fleet. Thereafter, and for centuries, Byzantine seapower held back the Arabs and the Turks from the northern Mediterranean, thus preserving the traditions of the ancient world long after Italy and the West had been overrun by barbarians. Constantinople became a great commercial center, though in later years its trade was increasingly carried in Arab or Italian bottoms. But its navy was always outstanding. Intricately organized under a proud admiral, who flaunted a gold-cloth hat and an orange and gold tunic displaying the portrait of the emperor, it was built around the dromon, a descendant of the classical galley. Rowed by as many as a hundred oars in two banks, the dromon often had two masts (fitted in later years with lateen sails), a fighting castle, and a ram. The Arab ship which opposed it, though more maneuvrable, was rather similar in design, since it, too, had been derived from the ancient galley. But the dromon had one great advantage : it was armed with Greek fire, a secret weapon which was an astonishing anticipation of modern weaponry.

Greek fire was a combustible mixture of naphtha, sulphur, and saltpeter, supposedly invented by a Syrian engineer, Callinicus. It was squirted at the enemy from the dromon's decks out of long tubes, launched in thin incendiary rockets, or splattered from clay jars thrown by catapults. The Arabs protected their ships with metal, their decks with sand, but it was of little use. Greek fire was a terrifying and effective weapon.

In the frequent naval encounters between Byzantium and the Arabs, Scandinavian mercenaries often manned the Byzantine ships against the Egyptian soldiers of Islam. Other Scandinavians from Sweden not only formed the Varangian bodyguard of the Emperor, but

26 *An Arab warship in the Indian Ocean
in the 16th century. These ships, derived from
the Mediterranean galley when the
conquering Arabs pushed westward to Spain,
changed little for centuries. The ship first
appeared in the Mediterranean, but
was independently developed around the world.
A great seafaring nation from earliest times,
the Chinese developed many types of
junks, built to sail with the monsoons.
27-32 A variety of rowing and sailing junks,
brightly painted fore and aft.
The largest junks often had four or five masts,
and 60 or more cabins.*

27
28
29

30
31
32

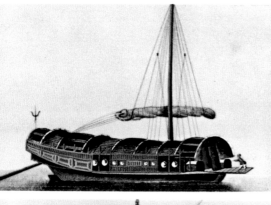

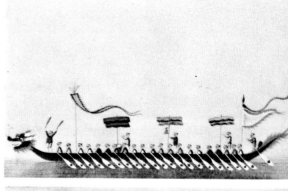

about 900 had laid the foundations of the Russian state. These Vikings, or "kings of the sea," were everywhere. In 911 a Viking invader named Rollo forced the king of France to grant him the fief of Normandy. In 1000 Leif Ericsson on his way to Greenland was driven by a storm onto the North American coast, leading to subsequent Viking exploration of America. A few years later Vikings from Normandy began to infiltrate into southern Italy, leading to the creation in the next century of a Norman kingdom in South Italy and Sicily. In 1034, while the Viking king Canute ruled England, Denmark, and Norway, down in the Mediterranean a certain Harald Hardrada was leading the Byzantine fleet against the Arab pirates. In 1066 this same Hardrada, now king of Norway, was defeated by King Harold of England at Stamford Bridge. Harold then marched south to meet his death at the hands of another Norman-Viking, William the Conqueror.

These Vikings were indeed everywhere— from Iceland to North Africa, from Russia to America. Superb seamen, they had begun as pirates, raiding, burning, looting, for glory, adventure, and wealth. As they grew more civilized and turned Christian they began to colonize in England, France and Italy, Iceland and Greenland, and even, some believe, on the mainland of North America. Their bleak Greenland settlements persisted for an incredible five centuries, right up to the time of Columbus.

The Vikings lived in and for their ships, which for beauty and seaworthiness have seldom been surpassed. Clinker-built, long and graceful, with shallow draught and high prow and stern posts, they were of several types.

Shortest and roundest was the *knorr*, or merchant vessel. The famous Oseberg and Gokstad ships, recovered from grave mounds, were coastal ships and were still small by Viking standards. The largest were the great warships, the *drakkars* (dragons) and *snekkars* (serpents), over 100 feet long with 60 to 80 oars and a multicolored square sail. These "long ships" boasted terrifying, gilded dragon heads at the prow—which by law had to be removed when entering home waters. Each district or village had its boat, under the command of a chief, or *jarl*, and when a raid was in prospect hundreds of ships would rendezvous for a night of feasting, fighting, dancing, and sacrifice to Odin and Thor before setting off all together for some distant coast. The Vikings seem to have navigated as much by instinct as by the stars or occasional landfalls.

The aged king Charlemagne wept in his beard at the sight of the Viking ships off his coasts. "I am overwhelmed with sadness at the thought of the harm they will do to my descendants and their subjects," he cried. He was right. And yet he was wrong, too, for the last Viking-Norman gathering of the "long ships" against England in 1066 helped to shape the modern world.

In a few hundred years the Viking ships which had brought William the Conqueror to England had evolved into the "round ship," broader and deeper in draught, and without oars. Rudimentary "castles" had appeared at either end, and a true rudder instead of a steering oar at the stern. Ships such as these, and the rather similar "Hansa cog" of the German trading towns, carried on a brisk

33 Naval warfare typical
of the Hundred Year's War
between France and England,
which saw the introduction
of cannon. The medieval
round ship, which fought in
this war and carried crusaders
to the Holy Land, was
ultimately derived from the
Viking "long ship."
34 A fanciful floating fortress,
drawn in 1483.
35 (Next page.)
Amphibious attack upon
a fortified town in the period
just after the Hundred Year's
War, from a miniature.

34

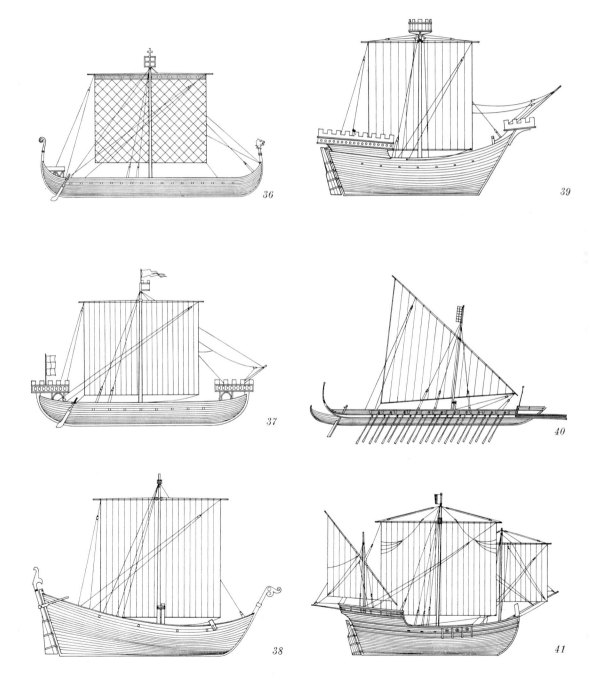

36

39

37

40

38

41

36 A "drakkar," or Viking warship.
37 English warship from the Cinque Ports,
   with fighting castles, 1284.
38 English round ship with stern rudder.
39 The Hansa cog, German, 14th century.
40 Mediterranean war galley with lateen sail,
   around 12th century.
41 A Spanish carrack of 15th century.
42 A Flemish carrack, 1470.
43 A caravel, early 15th century, much like Columbus's "Nina."
44 English galleon, "Henri Gráce à Dieu," of Henry VIII, 1545.
45 Typical galleon, late 16th century.
46 "La Réale," flagship of the French
   Mediterranean galley fleet during the 17th century.
47 Dutch "jacht" of the 17th century.

42

45

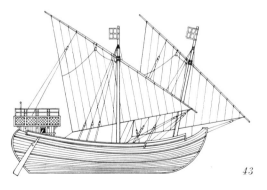

43

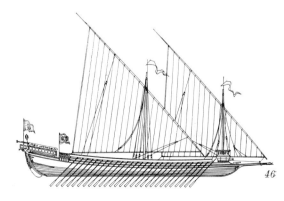

46

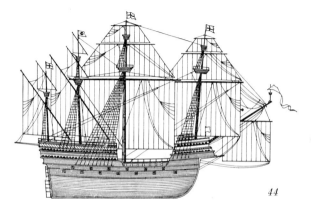

44

47

48 *15th century trading vessel, meticulously painted on stained glass, is one of merchant fleet built under Jacques Cœur, great finance minister, who restored French navy and commerce at end of the Hundred Years' War. He especially encouraged trade with the Levant and throughout the Mediterranean.*
49 *(Next page.) Henry VIII of England (standing in waist) sails for France in 1520 to meet Francis I on the Field of the Cloth of Gold. His ship, decked with golden sails, is the "Henri Grâce à Dieu" (Great Harry).*

commerce in the northern waters, manned by sailors such as the one described by Chaucer :

Hardy he was, and wys to undertake :
With many a tempest hadde his berd been shake;
He knew well al the havenes, as they were,
From Gootlond to the Cape of Fynystere . . .

And ships like these carried many of the crusaders toward the Holy Land in that curious series of expeditions, sometimes idealistic, more often sordid, which had such momentous consequences for the West. For the crusaders, untutored warriors from northern Europe, learned much from the superior civilizations of the Arab and the Byzantine, while the Italian city states—Venice, Genoa, Pisa—supplied money and troop transports to those crusaders who chose to go by sea, and warships to all of them, thus laying the foundations for their wealth and power during the Renaissance.

For almost two hundred years crusading fleets, often made up of Italian ships, plied the Mediterranean. Occasionally round ships from the north would appear, like that fleet of 164 ships, manned by Germans, Flemish, and Anglo-Normans, which in 1147 set out from England, passed through the Straits of Gibraltar and reached the coast of Syria without major losses. Greed, rivalry, and conquest motivated the crusaders as much as religious fervor, while the treacherous storms of the Mediterranean and the skill of Saracen warships often proved to be their undoing. During the Third Crusade, Richard I of England and Philip II of France, allied with Genoa and Pisa, sailed eastward together. In 1191, the

Christian fleet came up against an enormous three-masted Moslem warship (possibly an Arab "junk") which held 1,500 people including 800 warriors, and held off the entire fleet until it was finally rammed and sunk.

By the Fourth Crusade the glamour had gone. Europe was shocked when the western warriors, transported in Venetian ships, seized and sacked Constantinople in 1204, holding it for almost 60 years. As a reward, Venice was given a large part of the city and possessions all around the Aegean. The crusades proper ended with the two abortive expeditions of King Louis IX of France in 1248 and 1270. During the first one, transported in ships from Genoa, the king was captured in Egypt and had to be ransomed. During the second he died of the plague. Both Genoa and Venice built the ships for this last of the important crusades.

They were sordid, these crusades, and yet human, too. Often forgotten were the thousands of devout pilgrims who, in between the major campaigns, risked the long and dangerous voyage in French or Italian bottoms to visit the shrines of the Holy Land. The mingling of pilgrims, western adventurers, Italian merchants, Byzantine Greeks, and Arab warriors in rivalry, trade, war, and friendship during this extraordinary period did much for the advancement of civilization.

The more tangible results of the crusades—the Latin states in the eastern Mediterranean, including the holdings of the Hospitalers, the Knights of the Temple, and other chivalric orders—survived for some centuries. But the Italian states benefited most of all, especially Venice, the Queen of the Mediterranean. Her

possessions dotted the eastern Mediterranean, her merchant ships ranged widely, protected by the great war galleys mass-produced in the famous Arsenal. (In later years it could "prefabricate" a galley of 1001 pieces in two hours !) But in the fourteenth century, Venice, as well as Genoa, the Latin states, and Byzantium began to be threatened by a new power arising in the East, that of the Ottoman Turks.

The Turks began their meteoric career about 1300. In 1416 they first clashed with Venice, and in 1453 took Constantinople, battering down its walls with artillery, and ending 1,000 years of empire. Shortly thereafter they swept the Genoese out of the Aegean, and began to threaten Venice, provoking a major war which lasted, with interruptions, for two centuries, and soon widened out into a bitter struggle between the naval forces of Christendom and Islam for control of the Mediterranean. During the first half of the sixteenth century two figures dominated the contest, Khaireddin Pasha, or Barbarossa, the Turkish admiral (he was originally a Greek) and the great Genoese admiral, Andrea Doria. The climax came in 1571 at the battle of Lepanto, a ferocious melee between the Turkish galleys on one side, and those of the Holy League (Charles V, the Papacy, and Venice) on the other, well over 400 ships all told. Lepanto, the greatest naval battle since Actium, and the last major clash between galleys, was in a sense the culmination and end of the crusades ; Turks and other Moslems arrayed against Italians, French, Germans, Poles, and Hungarians. Although the Turks were soundly defeated, the results were indecisive. Nevertheless, after Lepanto the

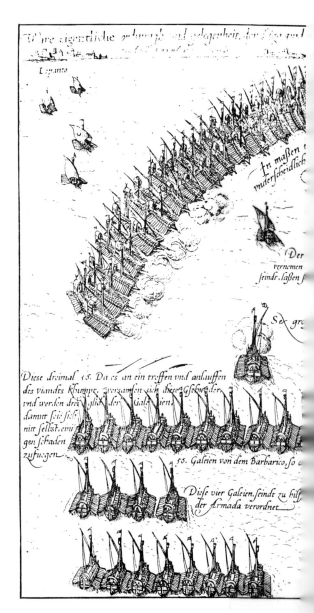

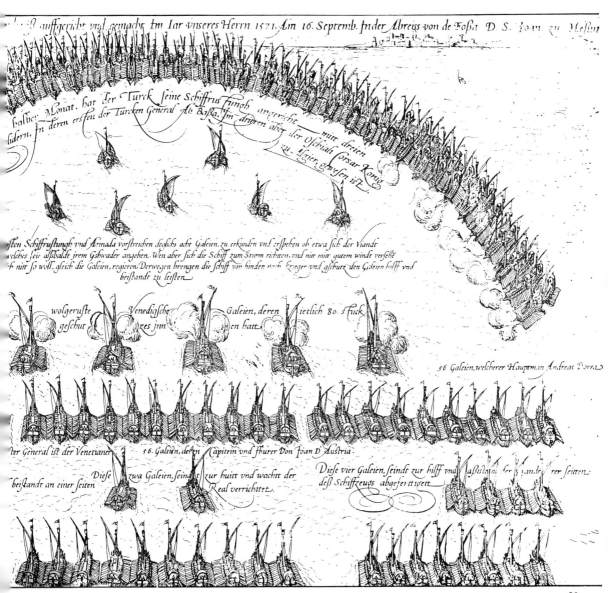

50

37

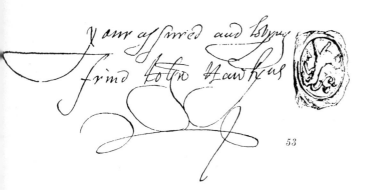

53

power both of the Turks and of Venice began to wane as the Dutch, French, and English began to cut into the trade of the Mediterranean and of the East.

The heady experiences of the crusades had helped to awaken Europe. Throughout the later Middle Ages, there was a stirring of new ideas and energies as the English for the first time began to think of themselves as Englishmen and the French as Frenchmen. As both countries groped toward nationhood they began to get in each other's way. There followed a long series of indecisive and exhausting engagements on land and sea, generally called the Hundred Years' War, which laid the foundations for England's mastery of the sea, and for France's absolutism. For the English found that they could not get at France without naval control of the Channel, while the French, whose land was cruelly ravaged during the wars, found they could not shake off the English grip without a strong central government.

France relied on a heterogeneous fleet gathered from Genoa, Spain, and elsewhere. In the opening engagement, off Sluys in 1340, the English fleet, led by Edward III and the great barons—Gloucester, Northampton, Warwick, Lancaster—smashed the French. Genoese crossbowmen were no match for English archers, while one English ship discharged crude cannon from her deck. The result : control of the Channel for over 30 years, and the great English victories of Crécy, Calais, and Poitiers, the capture of King John, the ravages of the Black Prince in the south of France, and in 1360 the humiliating peace of Brétigny. Then it was France's turn. Under the strong monarch, Charles V, the navy was reorganized and French seapower restored. While the great soldier, Bertrand du Guesclin, harassed the Black Prince in the south, the French fleet, reinforced by Mediterranean galleys and Castilian ships, regained control of the Channel at La Rochelle in 1372 and began to attack the coastal towns of England, which braced itself for an invasion that never came. By 1380 England had lost most of her possessions in France ; but France herself was in ruins.

The final phase of this savage, purposeless conflict began when the English, under Henry V, having regained control of the seas, defeated three times the number of French at Agincourt in 1415, reconquered Normandy, then until Henry's death in 1422 proceeded methodically to subdue France. A dark indecisive period followed—that of Jeanne d'Arc, the Dauphin, the Armagnacs against the Burgundians. In France's slow climb back to power the services of Jacques Cœur, the merchant prince of Bourges stand out. His motto was, "A cœur vaillant, rien d'impossible !" He reorganized the finances, providing the wherewithal to fight the war, created a new navy, resurrected Marseilles and St. Louis's port of Aigues-Mortes, and built up France's trade with the Mediterranean and Levant. And for this he was rewarded with disgrace and imprisonment. By the time of his death in 1456 the English held only Calais. A few years later, Louis XI, the Spider King, began France's reconstruction under a royal absolutism, while the English, turned inward for a time by the Wars of the Roses, emerged under the Tudors as a great seafaring nation.

54

55 *In ships such as this Columbus and his
successors explored the New World and the Orient
in the early 16th century. De Bry here allegorically
represents an early voyage to the West Indies.*

The great Age of Discovery, when the intrepid mariners of Europe first ventured across the inhospitable oceans in the fifteenth and sixteenth centuries, did not happen by chance. Bursting with vitality, Europe was searching for new markets, especially in the fabled Indies whose spices, rich fabrics, and perfumes had long been funneled westward by the merchants of Italy. But the eastern route through the Mediterranean and the Red Sea had now been closed by the rampaging Turks, putting Venice and Genoa into a slow decline. Besides, the restless merchants of the west coveted this rich trade for themselves. There was no longer any way to reach the Indies except by sea around the Cape of Africa, or perhaps even westward across the Atlantic to Cathay. If the earth was really round, as the Greek geographer Ptolemy had said, there would be little danger of falling off its edge. Indeed, a westward voyage might reach to the coasts of Asia and garner riches beyond belief. Here was reason enough for sailing boldly into the unknown seas.

Such a voyage would have been unthinkable a hundred years earlier with the clumsy little round ships of the north or the coastal galleys of the Mediterranean. But after a century of unparalleled development, the ships of Europe had become fully capable of mastering the open seas. The fruitful mingling of ideas and commerce of north and south and east, initiated with the crusades, had brought to fruition a new type of ship, best exemplified by the massive carrack, or its slimmer sister, the galleon, which combined the best elements from the Mediterranean and the north. The hull was sturdy,

56 A ship very similar to the "Santa Maria" of Columbus, in which he made his first voyage to the New World in 1492, is shown in a printer's mark from Antwerp dated 1487. Such ships were small but seaworthy.

57 Prince Henry the Navigator of Portugal, the earliest and greatest patron of overseas exploration. He actively studied navigation and the literature of exploration and sent his ships down the African coast and out to the islands of the Atlantic.

58 Prince Henry died in 1460. His work was carried on by King John II of Portugal, shown here in consultation with a visiting German scholar, Hieronimus Münzer.

59 The principle of the astrolabe, a navigation instrument, is illustrated here in a woodcut from a Portuguese treatise of 1509.

60 A depiction of the globe from the same book, showing the equatorial zone, which was thought uninhabitable.

60

57　58

59

61 *Christopher Columbus.*

like the northern merchantman, but showed the long lines of the galley. Square sails from the north, as well as lateen sails from the south for closer work into the wind, were spread upon the three or four masts—again a southern trait—while the stern rudder, which first appeared in the north, added a new element of control. Later, spritsails, topsails, and top-gallants were piled on for speed. Cannon lining the decks of this new ship (and later poking from gunports in its sides) ensured a necessary defense against Moslem pirates or northern freebooters—for there was still little distinction between merchantman and warship, and the seas belonged to the strongest. This was the ship of the explorers. By the middle of the fifteenth century it was to be found north and south, and remained basically unchanged for centuries thereafter.

To sail these great ships on the high seas, far from familiar landfalls or known winds, required new advances in the art of navigation. The compass, long known, was much improved while the hourglass and log were used to measure elapsed time and distance. But more than this was needed in the open ocean, and it was in the westward-facing Iberian peninsula, just emerging from the domination of the Moors, that the arts of navigation were most intensively studied, especially by Prince Henry of Portugal, the "Navigator," who set up a kind of seafaring academy on the rocky shores of Sagres Bay. Gathering around him a band of mariners and learned men, Christian, Jewish, and Moslem, he collected all the available information on the sea and distant lands, and sent out his ships west and south

in ever longer voyages from 1418 on. From the astrologers, then popular in the peninsula, he adapted much astronomical lore and a simplified astrolabe for "shooting the stars" for position, and worked out a system for determining latitudes in the southern hemisphere by the height of the sun. Winds, tides, and ocean currents were studied, manuals of navigation compiled, charts and maps much improved—for many of the explorers were cartographers as well.

Impelled by a fanatic nationalism, the Portuguese made tremendous efforts to keep their voyages and their methods secret. But in the end it proved impossible to keep the curtain lowered on their accomplishments; for in seafaring, if not in politics, it was an age of internationalism. The great Genoese admiral, Andrea Doria, for instance, served whoever would pay him best—the Italians, the French king, the Papacy, and finally Charles V in Spain. Discontented Portuguese like Magellan, who sailed westward for Spain in 1519, put their knowledge at the service of other nations. Columbus, another Genoese, was also employed by Spain after the Portuguese had refused to back him. Indeed the Italians, with their long maritime tradition, were everywhere. The Cabots served England; Verrazzano, France, while Amerigo Vespucci, who gave his name to America, was sent to the west both by Spain and by Portugal. And like the ships of the time, the ports were international. In the port of Antwerp, in the sixteenth century, as an example, sailors and merchants from England, Germany, Italy, Spain, and Portugal rubbed shoulders. In such

62   Ferdinand Magellan.

an atmosphere it was hard to keep any secrets.

The Portuguese, however, had been at the business of exploration for many years before the rest of Europe became aware of it. Isolated Portuguese ships may have reached America in the early fifteenth century, while French or Basque fishermen probably visited the Grand Banks in the same period. When the Portuguese under Prince Henry colonized the Madeiras and Azores in the 1420's-30's, and then started a systematic exploration of the West African coast, they found trading stations already established there by hardy, Viking-descended mariners from Dieppe on the Channel coast. (Jean Cousin from Dieppe may also have reached the mouth of the Amazon in 1488). Driving out the Dieppois, the Portuguese pushed slowly down the African coast. By 1445, they had rounded Cape Verde and had established a lively trade with West Africa, sending out about 25 caravels a year. By 1460, the year Prince Henry died, they had reached Sierra Leone. A new effort under King John II after 1481 saw Dias round the Cape of Good Hope, and Vasco da Gama reach India in 1498.

A true national effort, carried on with remarkable persistence, had at last brought Portugal to the fabled Indies. In 1500 a fleet of 13 ships under Cabral, first touching at Brazil to claim that country for Portugal, went on to start up the trade with India, returning to Lisbon with the first load of pepper and other spices. Three years later the price of pepper at Lisbon was only one fifth of what it was in Venice, since the Venetians had to buy it at inflated prices from the Arabs at Alexandria. Soon thereafter the Portuguese wrested control of the Indian seas from the Arabs, established a capital at Goa, opened trade with the East Indies, Siam, and China, and visited Japan in 1542. Their lucrative trade with the East, still a jealously guarded secret, could no longer be entirely concealed from the covetous eyes of other Europeans.

It may have been Columbus's idea to circumvent the Portuguese by sailing west around the world to Cathay and the Spice Islands; but being only partially privy to the secrets of the Portuguese navigators he grossly underestimated the distance. In the ups and downs of his four famous voyages (once he was returned to Spain a prisoner in chains), he managed to discover the West Indies, Venezuela, and Central America; but he died, it seems, in the belief that he had reached the outlying parts of Asia. The chief contribution of Columbus was not really the discovery of America but the fixing of the main routes to and from America by sea, the routes which were soon to be plied by the Spanish galleons carrying treasure from New Spain to Spain. His demonstration of how to reach the Americas, following upon the Portuguese successes to the south, began to awaken such an intense interest in Europe that the Pope himself, foreseeing a mad scramble for new lands and trade, decided to take a hand. He promulgated a bull, a year after Columbus's first voyage of 1492, which established a demarcation line from pole to pole through the Atlantic, allowing Spain rights of exploration and settlement to the west of it and Portugal to the east. Being a Spaniard, the Pope rather favored Spain, thus

63 A ship caught among icebergs in the northern
seas. Explorers in the 16th century were to be found
everywhere, from the Arctic to the tropics,
from the Americas to the East Indies.

leading to a private treaty between the two countries in 1494 which moved the line somewhat to the west, allowing Portugal to lay claim to Brazil in 1500.

After Columbus the Americas, although recognized for what they were, were still considered as a rather annoying barrier to the attainment of Asia beyond. Thus Spain dispatched Magellan in 1519 to find a passage through to Asia. He found one—the Straits of Magellan—and at one point spent 38 days beating his way about four miles through the narrows into the Pacific. Magellan himself was killed by natives in the Philippines, but his first officer brought the only surviving ship home around the world. While Magellan was setting off in 1519, Cortes the Conquistador was marching against the Aztec kingdom in Mexico. Its fall, with that of the Andean kingdom of the Incas at the hands of Pizarro after 1531, was to change the entire picture.

Forgotten now were the spices and perfumes of the Indies. With American gold, silver, and jewels flowing back to Spain, she grew rich and her shipping began to dominate Europe. The triumphs of Portugal in the Indian Ocean, never much publicized, were thrown into the shade by the fabulous tales of the golden empires of Mexico and Peru. This time the covetous eyes of Europe began to watch the Spaniards as well as the Portuguese.

One of the first to protest the Papal bull of 1493 supporting the Spanish and Portuguese monopoly in the New World was Francis I of France, who was anxious to strengthen the lagging seapower of his country. Although he gave out countless letters of marque to the hardy mariners of the north and west coasts of France, who were passionately interested in the New World, he was vacillating in his support, often repudiating them altogether. Nevertheless the mariners of Dieppe, of Brouage, of La Rochelle continued to send out their little fleets to Brazil, to Newfoundland, to Sumatra, capturing Spanish or Portuguese galleons when they could but more often ending up on the gallows of Lisbon or Seville ; for the Spanish and Portuguese defended their monopoly with ferocity. In 1516 the Portuguese wiped out the French outposts in Brazil with atrocious brutality, and in 1565 the Spaniards massacred the French colonists in Florida.

Greatest of the northern mariners was Jean Ango of Dieppe, half sea dog, half humanist scholar, who set up a miniature sea academy like that of Prince Henry in his Florentine-style palace, and at one time commanded a private fleet of 30 corsairs which he dispatched all over the world. In 1524 the Florentine, Giovanni da Verrazzano, in Ango's service, explored the coastline of North America. A few years later he was in Brazil. Surprised by the natives, he was massacred and eaten in sight of his ships. Between 1534 and 1541 the Breton, Jacques Cartier, reconnoitered the St. Lawrence for Francis I, but the French did not return there until the seventeenth century ; for Francis and his successors, beset by foreign wars and later by the civil wars at home, and by the implacable opposition of the Spanish and Portuguese, never gave enough support to their explorers. In one of Francis's many attempts to establish his seapower he negotiated between wars with Henry VIII of

England at the field of the Cloth of Gold near Calais. Henry, always the showman, arrived in a magnificent ship with golden sails, the *Great Harry*. England's fleet was already a power to be reckoned with.

In the end it was the English and the Dutch who destroyed the Spanish-Portuguese monopoly, but not for many years. The English, at first avoiding a conflict, made a series of brave attempts to find a passage to Cathay east or west around the top of the world. As early as 1497 and 1498 John Cabot, a wealthy Italian who had settled in England, and his son Sebastian sailed under the patronage of that shrewd businessman, Henry VII, to Labrador, Newfoundland, and Nova Scotia. Cabot was sure that he had found the country of the "Great Khan," but when he returned without spices or gold, England and its king lost interest. Henry VIII, often called the Father of the Royal Navy, was more concerned with building up his fleet at home; but the idea of finding a passage northeast or northwest to Asia never died. In 1553 and 1554 Sir Hugh Willoughby and Richard Chancellor sailed north in an attempt to beat eastward around the top of Russia. Both eventually lost their lives, but not before they had opened up Russia to English trade and exploration. In the 1570's and '80's the stubborn English tried again to find Cabot's northwest passage, Sir Martin Frobisher and John Davis penetrating as far as Baffin Land and the Hudson and Davis Straits. Sir Humphrey Gilbert took possession of Newfoundland for the English in 1583, but lost his life on the return journey. He was last seen on his laboring frigate "sitting abaft with

a booke in his hand" crying out gaily : "We are as neere to heaven by sea as by land."

After the middle of the century the English, growing bolder, began to tangle with the Spanish, raiding their treasure ships and settlements in the Atlantic and Caribbean. In the 1560's, Sir John Hawkins, a tough free-booter with a liking for money, ran afoul of the Spanish when he began selling African slaves in the West Indies. Later he became the respected treasurer of the Queen's navy, building and arming the ships that fought the Armada. The archetype of the British gentleman-freebooter was Sir Francis Drake, who made a profession of baiting the Spanish. Nephew of Hawkins, he served under him as a young man. In 1572, sacking the Spanish town of Nombre de Dios, he returned to England and used the plunder to organize an expedition of five ships to prey upon the Spanish in the Pacific, where no Englishman had been before. A cruel voyage through the Straits of Magellan brought him into the great sea, where he captured several galleons and sailed north to California. Eventually he made his way across the Pacific, around the world, arriving back at Plymouth in 1580 with his one surviving vessel. "Arise, Sir Francis, Vice-Admiral of my fleet," cried Queen Elizabeth as she knighted him aboard his ship.

Drake continued his depredations against the Spanish. In 1586 he sacked Santo Domingo and Cartagena in the Caribbean ; the next year, with 30 ships, he ranged the Spanish coast itself with impunity, destroying a quantity of shipping in Cadiz harbor. The Spanish reacted slowly (Philip II, their king, who was

64 A "marvellous meteor"
seen by explorers off
Novaya Zemlya in 1596.

subject to seasickness, was extremely lethargic in naval matters), but this was too much. The war became official, and in 1588 the Spanish sailed north for England with an armada of unprecedented size—132 ships, crammed with 30,000 soldiers and sailors, and mounting 3,165 cannon—to seize control of the Channel in preparation for an invasion. The English, forewarned, sallied out from Plymouth with a fleet of 102 ships and half the number of men. But these ships were of the best. "Certes," wrote a contemporary "there is no prince in Europe that hath a more beautiful or gallant sort of ships than the Queen's majesty of England... for strength, assurance, nimbleness, and swiftness of sailing, there are no vessels in the world to be compared with ours." And they were commanded by those vigorous sea dogs, Drake, Hawkins, and Frobisher, under Lord Howard of Effingham as admiral. The seas, the winds, the sheer cumbersomeness of their fleet was against the Spaniards. The Armada was broken up, and what was left was destroyed by storms. The decline of Spain's seapower was now evident to all of Europe.

The English had had a lot to do with it; but so had the Dutch. These industrious seamen, so much of whose land was water, began to chafe under the rule of Spain. For centuries they had been fishermen of cod and herring, which not only brought them wealth but taught them the arts of shipbuilding and navigation. The freighting of goods in their seaworthy vessels brought them even more wealth. Their first protests against Spanish rule were ruthlessly suppressed by the Spanish Duke of Alva, which merely strengthened their resolve. In the 1570's these "beggars of the sea," as the Spaniards contemptuously called them, and the Dutch gloried in the name, began a long guerrilla warfare, their light boats dodging in and out of the bays and inlets of their watery land, which by the end of the century, with some help from England, had brought virtual independence to the United Provinces. Last of the great maritime nations to emerge, the Dutch now began, and with a vengeance, the old game of baiting the Spaniards and the Portuguese from one end of the world to the other, helped out by the English and the rapacious Barbary pirates of North Africa, successors of Khaireddin. In concert with the English they went after the weakening empire of the Portuguese, penetrating and then virtually taking over the rich East Indian trade. They even sent out explorers, one giving his name to the Barents Sea, another, an Englishman in their employ, to the Hudson River.

Times were changing. Exploration was giving way to trading companies and colonization. The Dutch East India Company was founded in 1602, the English East India Company two years before. As early as 1555 England's Muscovy Company had been created, as a result of the voyages of Willoughby and Chancellor, to trade with Russia. There had been many attempts to plant colonies, notably the two "lost" Virginian colonies of Sir Walter Raleigh and John White in the 1580's. With the weakening of the Spanish and Portuguese empires, the rivalries of other European nations, on the high seas and in all parts of the world, were to determine the course of history in the succeeding centuries.

65 *Fire and destruction mark battle of 1666
during second Anglo-Dutch War. For a century
and a half, in home seas and abroad, the rising
powers of Europe fought each other for mastery
of the seas. Finally England emerged supreme.*

Cardinal Richelieu was most anxious to build up the French navy. Echoing his sentiments, one of his subordinates wrote in 1626, "Whoever commands the sea will have great power on the land. Look at the King of Spain. After he had mastered the seas he was able to conquer so many kingdoms that the sun will never set on his possessions !'' Spain (following Portugal) had certainly shown the way ; but the Dutch shattered the waning naval power of Spain at the Battle of the Dunes in 1639, and thereafter the struggle on the seas became a confusing, many-sided contest among all the great powers of Europe.

Throughout the seventeenth and eighteenth centuries there was almost continuous fighting on the seas—much of it bloody and cruel, and all of it apparently quite senseless. The history books present us with a bewildering succession of naval encounters in Europe and in the colonies, most of them reflections of equally bewildering land wars with odd names, such as the War of the League of Augsburg, the War of the Spanish Succession, the War of Jenkins' Ear. These wars were fought, they tell us, because of dynastic rivalries, religious differences, or sheer lust for power—which hardly seems to explain either their frequency or their ferocity. Toward the end of the eighteenth century the murky picture begins to clear a bit as two great powers emerge—England on the seas, and Napoleon's France on land. And England, with its command of the seas, wins. Then we begin to understand. Seapower, during these centuries, was the vital factor in the spread of European power around the globe. The exiled Napoleon, brooding on St. Helena, was heard

66 The "Sovereign of the Seas," launched
in 1637, was the largest, most heavily
armed, and most lavishly decorated warship
of her day. The Dutch, who often
encountered her in battle, called her "The
Golden Devil," because she glittered
with gilded carving from stem to stern.
Built by master-shipwrights Peter
and Phileas Pett for Charles I of England,
she was paid for out of the Ship Money
tax, which helped bring on the English
Civil War. She was a three-decker with
100 guns, measuring 127 feet along the keel.

to mutter, "Ah! If I had only been master of the seas. . . ."

Seapower, of course, meant more than just a navy. It meant a strong merchant marine, an active commerce, flourishing colonies, a string of way stations around the world, and, last but not least, a navy to keep the sea lanes open and to protect the colonies and mother country from attack. Naturally, each nation wanted these things for itself, and since colonization and trade were matters of who got there first with the greatest strength, conflicts were inevitable. First to profit from the decline of Spain and Portugal were the Dutch. The Dutch East India Company, as an instrumentality of the government, rapidly displaced the Portuguese in the Indies, colonizing the Cape of Good Hope as a way station, and pushing the weaker English into the backwater of India. From their bases in the Spice Islands the Dutch pushed on to Japan, where for many years they alone were allowed trading privileges. By 1625 the industrious Dutch were trading with France, England, Venice, the Barbary coast, and the Levant. Every year 16 whalers were sent to Greenland, eight ships to Russia, 20 to Guinea, and 60 to the Indies. After the founding of the Dutch West India Company in 1621, Admiral Piet Heyn made inroads in Brazil (in 1628 he captured the richest Spanish treasure fleet to date); a number of West Indian islands were seized; and colonies were planted on the North American coast—including New Amsterdam (New York), purchased from the Indians in 1626 for 24 dollars (60 guilders).

Such far-flung, bustling prosperity aroused jealousy and alarm among Holland's rivals,

for by this time the upholding of national interests on the sea by the nations of Europe had become almost an obsession. By the time of Cromwell, England possessed a powerful navy, though she still trailed the Dutch in merchant shipping. Her North American colonies, however, had begun to flourish— Jamestown in Virginia, founded in 1607, Plymouth of the "Pilgrims" (1620), Massachusetts Bay, which after 1630 attracted thousands of settlers, and finally William Penn's Philadelphia of 1682. New York was seized from the Dutch in 1664. In the East, England acquired Bombay in 1661 and began to take over the Dutch spice trade. There was reason enough for rivalry between the English and the Dutch on the seas.

The great naval wars between the two began in 1652 and lasted, with intervals, for over 20 years. These were sanguinary conflicts —as befitted two great powers contesting for supremacy on the world's seas—and were fought by powerful and ruthless admirals on both sides: Maarten Tromp, and his son Cornelis; the great Michiel de Ruyter, who dominated the later wars; and for the English such men as Robert Blake. Few of the engagements were decisive, though the low point came for the English in 1667 when de Ruyter sailed into the Thames estuary, throwing London into a panic, fired most of the English fleet, and captured its flagship, Royal Charles. England might well have succumbed to the Dutch had it not been for the leadership of the Duke of York, later James II, and for the untiring efforts of that garrulous diarist, Samuel Pepys, who as Secretary of the Admiralty

THILE

MER SEPTENTRIONALLE

LANDE

ESCO
SSE

Les orcades

Mer Germanique

GROVLLANT

NOROVAGVE

GOTHIE

SVECE

LAPONIE

FINLANDE

Moscovie

CORELIA

RUSSIA
ALBA

Sinus Granduicus

67

68

69

LE SOLEIL ROYAL

LE SOLEIL ROYAL

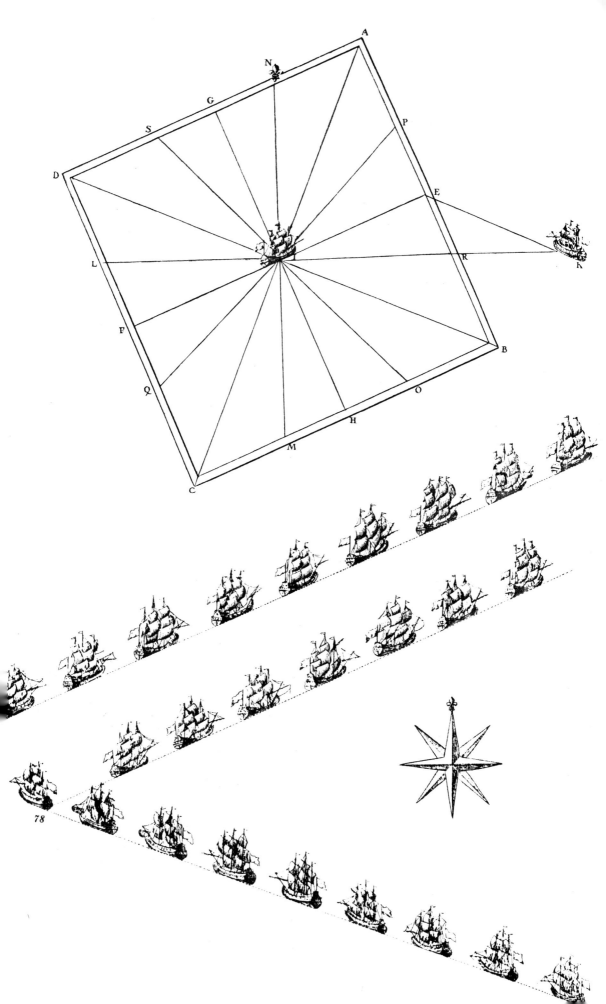

78

not only found the money to build the needed ships but reformed and regularized the entire administration of the Royal Navy, laying the basis for its future greatness.

France had had great periods on the sea but had never, because of apathy at home and constant internal troubles, maintained that continuity of purpose which was to bring England's seapower to the fore. In the first half of the seventeenth century Cardinal Richelieu had bravely tried to build up the French marine, but without lasting results. When Jean Baptiste Colbert came to power in the 1660's he found the navy almost nonexistent, and surveys indicated that France had only about 400 seaworthy merchant ships to some 4,000 for England and 16,000 for Holland. Since Louis XIV was as apathetic in naval matters as Philip II had been, Colbert despaired of catching up. "In England," he wrote, "they ridicule us as a people incapable of taking to the sea." Yet by the time of his death in 1683 Colbert had accomplished wonders. After he had borrowed ideas from the Dutch and English and even imported specialists in the trade, French shipbuilding (if not seamanship) became the finest in the world. He created a powerful navy, including a force of coastal galleys, improved the lot of the common sailor, and reorganized the officers' corps ; he fortified the harbors of Toulon, Rochefort, Le Havre, Brest, and Dunkerque, and built up a merchant fleet of some 4,000 units. He encouraged colonization, planting the first French factories in India and outposts in Guiana and Madagascar, while La Salle, with his support, extended the frontiers of

New France from Canada to the Mississippi. France, since the decline of Holland, was now second to England on the seas.

The first triumph of Colbert's new fleet was over the Dutch in the Mediterranean in 1676, Admiral Duquesne opposing the valiant Michel de Ruyter, who was killed in action. In 1690 the fleet under Tourville defeated the English and Dutch at Beachy Head, but could not achieve Louis XIV's purpose of returning James II to the throne of England. In the early eighteenth century, as the French fleet declined again, England emerged supreme on the seas in a series of wars with France and Spain in which she developed the art of blockading the fleets of her enemies while seizing colony after colony. At the Treaty of Utrecht in 1713 England acquired Gibraltar, Minorca, Newfoundland, and Acadia. By the end of the Seven Years' War in 1763 the French had been soundly defeated around the world, and England had fallen heir to the greater part of the French empire in North America. At the same time the French had been driven out of India. England had become not only master of the seas, but the greatest of colonial powers.

England's triumph had been won by using her superior fleet in displays of power, for by the eighteenth century sea battles were often formalized affairs in which a clean-cut victory could only be achieved with difficulty. Opposing fleets faced each other in perfectly formed lines, sometimes as much as five miles long, watching for the chance to break the enemy's line with a thunderous broadside. The battle might be preceded by days of maneuvering to

gain the most advantageous position, guided by complex signals from the admiral (flags by day, fires by night). In this stilted chess game the ships themselves were positioned according to rates—a first rate ship had over 90 guns, a second over 80, and so forth—while the lighter frigates hovered at the rear. War, as on land, had become a game, and it was played for the game's sake by professionals; for the navies of Europe had become highly organized. The officers were gentlemen from professional navy families. The sailors (sometimes as many as 1,300 were crammed into a man-of-war) were often as not forced into service by press-gangs, and led a miserable life, suffering from bad food, scurvy, and inadequate living quarters.

The ships themselves had changed little in fundamentals since the sixteenth century (and there would be little change until the nineteenth century). The "castles" fore and aft had been lowered into the sweeping lines of the two or three decks, and the whole craft had become heavier and deeper to provide a steady platform for the cannon. The highly decorated stern of the seventeenth century (those windows were for the officers' cabins, including their latrines) had become simpler by the eighteenth. A special type of warship was the French galley of the Mediterranean coast (celebrated in Les Misérables), its low, graceful lines and elaborate gilt decoration concealing the misery within, for the galleys were rowed by convicts, slaves, and prisoners of war, usually five to each huge oar, condemned to a lifetime of labor, often sitting up to their waists in water, chained to their posts, covered with vermin, whipped to spur them on, and tossed overboard

when they died at the oar. The ordinary galley, with 26 oars, had 260 oarsmen, while the flagship, or Réale, had 462. By contrast, the proud officers of the galley corps came from the noblest families of Provence and were specialists in individual combat. Unable to compete with the man-of-war, the galley died out in the eighteenth century.

While the major battles on the seas grew more formal, there were many smaller engagements of a different character. The Americans, for instance, revere the naval officer, John Paul Jones, for his brilliant victory, in his Bonhomme Richard, over two British ships, and his raiding of the English coasts during the American Revolution. Meantime the ancient pastime of freebooting continued to flourish during the seventeenth and eighteenth centuries. At times it was hard to tell the difference between a privateer, with letters of marque authorizing him to prey upon enemy shipping, and the out-and-out pirate, who chose his victims to suit himself. The buccaneer, who infested the Caribbean during the seventeenth century, was somewhere in between. Sir Henry Morgan, greatest of the brethren, captured Panama in 1671 and ended up a respectable Deputy Governor of Jamaica. Among privateers, the French still tell of the great Jean Bart, who was honored by Louis XIV for his colorful exploits. In a class by themselves were the Barbary pirates of the North African coast who terrorized the Mediterranean for centuries, torturing and killing Christians with refined brutality.

Despite constant warfare on the high seas, ocean trade during the eighteenth century reached a new peak, revolutionizing the life of Europe. There was tea to drink in England and coffee in France. Men began to wear comfortable shirts of cotton, and women to dress in elaborate colored fabrics from the East, while both sexes for the first time began to sleep in nightshirts. The seventeenth century had carried its wares in small merchantmen of 150 to 200 tons, belonging to simply organized groups of private adventurers. Now great East Indiamen, some as large as 1,000 tons and armed to the teeth, plied regularly between Asia and Europe in the service of the big East India companies, which were almost states in themselves. In France, with its inconstant attitude toward the sea, the trading companies were never very profitable; but in England and Holland it was a different story. During the eighteenth century the British East India Company had become, in effect, the government of India. It had its own army and navy, its own flag, and a fleet of over 100 merchantmen, some the largest then afloat. Such companies, for the first time, issued stock, thus allowing the smallest investor or businessman to take an interest in their affairs and share in the profits. Under such stimulus, shipbuilding had become a science. Rope factories and foundries proliferated, ships were designed by engineers with meticulous care, while the best stands of trees were "nationalized" to provide the timber and masts for men-of-war.

Two of the most lucrative trades of the period were slaving and fishing. The traffic in negro slaves was a byproduct of the age of exploration. Started by the Portuguese, it was continued by the Spanish and French, and although outlawed by most nations in the late eighteenth and early nineteenth centuries, it continued for some time. The mortality on the slavers, heavily armed against frequent uprisings, was frightful, the unfortunate blacks being manacled between decks with scarcely room to move except during periods of enforced "dancing" on deck under the threat of the lash. But the occasional cargoes that got through paid enormous dividends. Of the many types of fishing practised by the northern nations, whaling was the most profitable. For almost 500 years the tough Basque sailors enjoyed a monopoly of whaling. In the late seventeenth century the Dutch and English captured the trade, only to be supplanted by the New Englanders of America a century later. From earliest times—perhaps before Columbus—the whalers had been exploring the northern and arctic seas in search of their huge prey. But in the eighteenth century more purposeful explorers, with government backing, filled in the last remaining blanks in the map of the Pacific—notably Louis Antoine de Bougainville, who discovered several Pacific islands, and Captain James Cook, one of England's greatest seamen, who in his three voyages after 1768 defined most of Australia, New Zealand, the Pacific islands, and the northwest coast of America. Cook was killed by Hawaiians in 1779.

In the mid-eighteenth century, after 100 years of warfare on the seas, England's triumph seemed assured. But when the American colonies revolted in 1775, a new period of adversity set in. Led by the French, whose fleet was again at the peak of its power,

80 Horatio Nelson, victor of Trafalgar. He destroyed Napoleon's fleet at the Battle of the Nile in 1798, was victorious at Copenhagen in 1801, then sealed the fate of Napoleon at Trafalgar by winning naval supremacy.

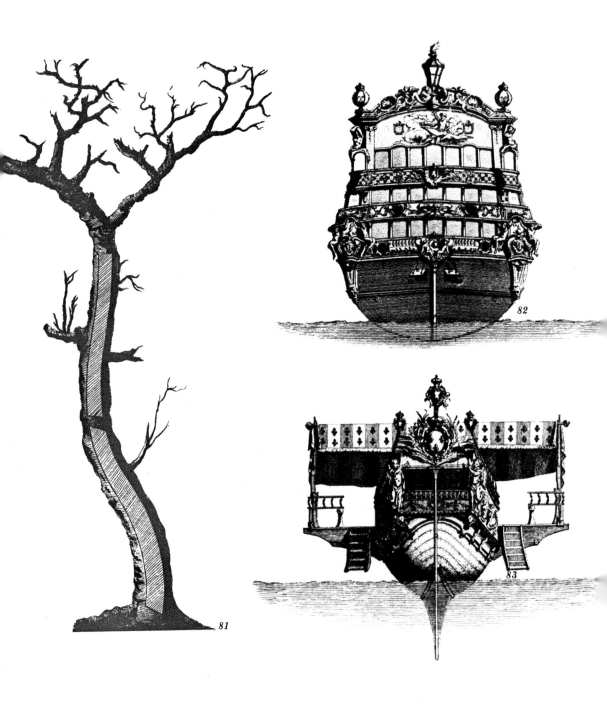

81

82

83

81 Shipbuilding in the
18th century became a science.
Shipwrights became engineers
and trees were "nationalized"
by the government to obtain
the best cuts for naval yards.
82 Decorated stern of a French
vessel of the first rank.
83 The poop of a "réale" or
galley flagship. France's
Mediterranean fleet of
galleys, lavishly decorated
on the outside, were rowed
by lifetime convicts and
slaves who lived in misery.
84 Stern of the "Etonnant" of
1802. France's fleet, ruined
by the revolution, was no
match for the ships of England.

84

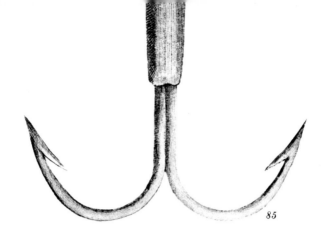

85

England's ancient enemies turned upon her, the French and Dutch harassing her both in Europe and in the West Indies. In 1781 two French fleets set out from Brest. One, under Pierre André de Suffren sailed boldly east, defeated the British in several encounters, and might have taken over India had not the peace intervened. The other, under Admiral de Grasse, turned up in the Chesapeake and with the backing of the Spanish, enforced a brief blockade of the British forces which helped to bring about the surrender of Cornwallis at Yorktown.

The French revolution, later in the century, left England, with its powerful fleet, once again opposing the military and naval might of all of Europe. But the Spanish and the Dutch fleets were shadows of their former selves, while the superb French fleet, with most of its senior officers executed or exiled, had fallen on hard times. In 1793 France declared war on England and in 1795 overran Holland, setting up the Batavian Republic (whereupon England seized the Dutch colonial empire). Although plagued by naval mutinies in 1797, the British fleet under Sir John Jervis easily defeated the dispirited Spanish at Cape St. Vincent. Napoleon, just coming into power, began to realize that British seapower was his real enemy. For several years he toyed with the idea of an invasion across the Channel, building up a force of barges at Boulogne, but in the end he knew that against the seapower of England he stood no chance. Perhaps British resistance could be undermined by a threat to India and the vital eastern trade, he thought. The result was the disastrous Egyptian compaign, which

brought the great British admiral Horatio Nelson into prominence. Egypt was seized in 1798, but what was left of the once-great French fleet was utterly dispersed by Nelson at the Battle of the Nile (or Abukir Bay). The French armies were bottled up in Egypt and eventually defeated. "If it had not been for you English, I should have been Emperor of the East," Napoleon said later.

Nelson went on to the bombardment of Copenhagen in 1801, and finally the climactic Battle of Trafalgar in 1805, in which he defeated the French and Spanish, regained unchallenged mastery of the seas, but lost his own life. The war continued on for another ten years, while England strangled the power of the continent with her blockading fleets and seized more of the colonies of Napoleon's unwilling allies, Spain and Holland. In 1812 the United States, irritated by England's ruthless treatment of neutrals, declared war on her—a most unnecessary little war which saw small naval engagements from the Great Lakes to the English Channel. Noteworthy was the emergence of the powerful American frigates, larger than any in the world, which distinguished themselves in individual combat. The first were the *United States* and the *Constitution*, both launched in 1797. Frigates such as these also carried out a pocket war against the Barbary pirates of Tunis in 1803. When the war of 1812 was over, and Napoleon had been safely exiled to St. Helena, a new period dawned, the long-lived "Pax Britannica". It was a peace based upon the dominance of British seapower throughout the known world.

85 *By the 18th century all the*
great maritime nations of
Europe were fishing the waters
of the world on a large scale.
Holland's prosperity was built
on its fisheries. France for
a long time specialized in cod.
86 *Fishing methods in the 18th*
century. Of the many types
of fishing, whaling was the
most profitable, taking the
fleets well up into polar
waters. First whalers were
the Basque, but by the 18th
century England and Holland
had captured the trade. At
the end of the century the
Americans became very active.

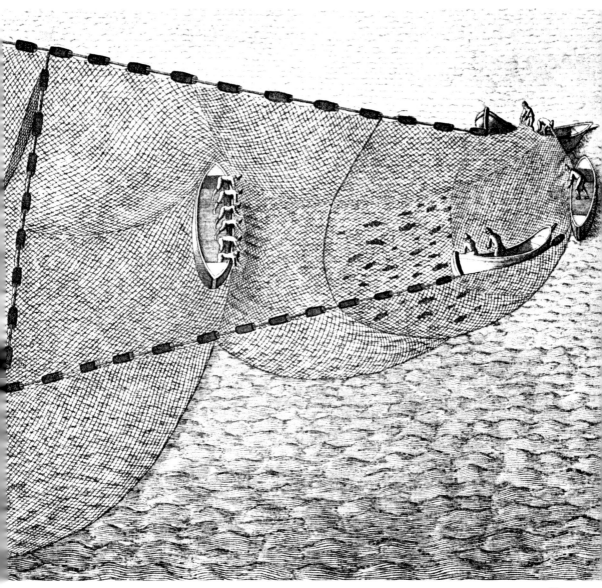

86

87 *The steamboat was born on the rivers and lakes of Europe and the United States while the sailing ship still ruled the seas. In the early 19th century it crept out into the stormy oceans. Today it is everywhere supreme.*

Since the best of the sailing ships were subject to the inconstancy of the winds, it is not surprising to find that through the centuries there were many proposals for the substitution of a steadier, more reliable source of energy. The favorite device was the paddlewheel, moved by beasts of burden or by human muscle. Examples come from China, the Roman Empire, and the Middle Ages. In 1798, when Napoleon was considering an invasion of England, one inventor proposed a "floating fortress," a huge raft with paddlewheels turned by windmills at each corner. England's men-of-war would have made short work of it!

When the steamboat made its first appearance during the eighteenth century it was almost as crude a device as this one, and as little noticed ; for unlike the sailing ship, which had undergone a gradual evolution, it was created by mechanics and inventors, by landlubbers in fact, and was a byproduct not of the sea but of the industrial revolution. Honest mariners scorned and feared it, and for years it stayed close to the rivers where it was born, far from the dangerous and tumultuous seas where ships-of-the-line fought the important battles and the great East and West Indiamen plied the trade routes of the world. Then gradually the steamboat crept out into the oceans, making a place for itself first in the passenger trade, where regularity was a virtue, then in the larger navies by the middle of the nineteenth century, and finally in the cargo trade, dominated until that time by the clipper, last and most magnificent of sailing ships. With the disappearance of the clipper, the end of the 5,000-year-old sailing era was in sight.

88

89

93

97

98

91   *92*

95   *96*

100   *101*

102　Two fast clipper ships, the "Ariel" and "Taeping," loaded with tea from Foo Chow in China, race up the English Channel in 1866. Both had left China together on *May* 30, had arrived in the Channel together 99 days later. The magnificent clippers, both British and American, were built for speed and represented the apogee of the sailing ship. The opening of the Suez Canal, only three years after the race depicted here, made the clipper obsolete, opening the era of steam.

The steam engine was the device that gave power and drive to the industrial revolution. Since the steamboat was built around an engine, its development had to wait upon that of its power plant. Newcomen's first "atmospheric" engine of around 1700 was too heavy and too weak to power a boat, and one can assume the same for Denis Papin's "cooking pot," which he invented about the same time, apparently for use in a paddlewheel boat. But this we will never know, because when jealous mariners destroyed a prototype of his boat in 1707, Papin gave up. After James Watt's invention of the first real steam engine around 1770, there were more attempts in France to adapt it to a boat. The Counts of Auxiron and Follenay built a steamboat, but it was sunk in the Seine (perhaps again by alarmed boatmen) before it could be tested. It was Count Jouffroy d'Abbans who in 1783 first demonstrated a practical steamboat. Watched by thousands of spectators, his *Pyroscaphe* successfully breasted the current of the Saône for an historic 15 minutes, then went on to further triumphs while he sought government support. But opposition from the Academy of Sciences (which was then supporting Montgolfier's pioneer balloon experiments) forced him to drop the project.

America soon took the lead from France. With its enormous distances, poor roads, and abundant rivers, it needed the steamboat. As early as the 1760's the industrialist, William Henry, tried to launch a steamboat on the Conestoga River, and in 1802 the brilliant Oliver Evans of Philadelphia, one of the first to invent a high-pressure engine, built a monster

amphibious steam dredge which made slow progress under its own power both on land and on water. About the same time John Stevens was responsible for some propeller-driven boats, then in 1808 made the first "sea voyage" from New York to Delaware with his paddlewheel *Phoenix*. But the greatest of the pioneers were Fitch and Fulton, who formed an interesting contrast. While Robert Fulton was both an admirable engineer and an adroit businessman, John Fitch was unstable, impractical, and always in trouble. Yet he got there first with a series of boats propelled by mechanical paddles at the sides or the stern, one of which ran a regular service on the Delaware during the summer of 1790, covering more than 2,000 miles. But Fitch was a self-defeating man. After years of poverty and distress, he committed suicide in 1798.

It was Fulton, with an ability to pick and choose among the best ideas of his time, who finally turned the steamboat from a gadget into a practical form of transportation. He was much influenced (as was Fitch) by the work of William Henry, and in 1793 went to England expressly to talk engines and boats with such pioneers as Watt and Boulton. In France after 1797 he produced a practical little submarine, the *Nautilus* (propelled by sail above the water and by a hand-cranked screw beneath), and in 1802 formed an association with Robert Livingston, the American minister at Paris (not only rich but an inventor himself) to build steamboats for America, In 1803 they successfully tested a little steamboat on the Seine, then ordered engine parts from Watt and Boulton and returned to America to build the famous

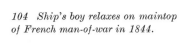

Clermont. At first it was called "Fulton's
Folly," but when the *Clermont* made its maiden
voyage up the Hudson to Albany and back in
August 1807 (32 hours upstream, 30 returning)
there were no doubters left. As Fulton wrote,
"The power of propelling boats by steam is
now fully proved." On October 1 the *Clermont*
began a regular New York—Albany service,
carrying as many as 100 passengers at a time.

Steam navigation spread rapidly in the
United States. Lake Champlain saw the first
lake steamer in 1809. The *New Orleans* of
Fulton, Livingston, and Nicholas Roosevelt
began service on the Mississippi in 1812, and by
1822 the river and its tributaries could boast
35 steamers, with their characteristic shallow
draught, high funnels, and huge wheels and
balance arms. In Europe, with its developed
communications, steam navigation caught on
more slowly. There were isolated experiments.
In Scotland in the 1780's Patrick Miller
equipped two of his double-hulled paddlewheel
boats with engines by William Symington, and
another went into the steam tug *Charlotte
Dundas* in 1802. Commercial service really
began with Henry Bell's *Comet*, which began
running from Glasgow to Greenock on the
Clyde in 1812. He charged three to four
shillings for the trip. There were 15 steamboats
on the Clyde by 1815, and many more throughout Britain. France, which had seen the first
steamboat, was way behind, with only 82
steamers by 1835 to Britain's 500. But by this
time steamboats had spread to all the lakes
and rivers of Europe and had even ventured
on the oceans. In 1816 the little steamer *Elise*
made a perilous, storm-tossed, 17-hour trip

across the Channel, sailing up the Seine to
receive a hero's welcome at Paris. Three years
later a full-rigged ship, the American *Savannah*,
with auxiliary engine and paddlewheels, crossed
the Atlantic and returned. She used her engines
very little: but still, steam had been introduced
onto the high seas.

But the sailing ship still ruled the oceans,
and the steamboat took little part in the great
events of the first half of the nineteenth
century. The great powers of Europe, exhausted after the Napoleonic struggle, were
determined to maintain the status quo, and
used their powerful sailing fleets to intimidate
potential troublemakers by "showing the flag"
or even resorting to a bombardment or a minor
war if necessary. Occasionally the fleets would
indulge in an adventure. In 1827 the combined
fleets of France, Britain, and Russia crushed
the Turks at the Battle of Navarino to secure
the independence of Greece. In 1830 the French
attacked Algiers across the Mediterranean and
began to carve out a new empire, while the
established colonial powers—especially England and Holland (to whom Britain had
returned the East Indies after the war)—
consolidated their own extensive empires,
maintaining trade and communications by
means of handsome East Indiamen, which by
this time were hardly distinguishable from the
naval frigates of the day.

During this period the graceful little ships
of New England began to appear in all the
seas, shipping cod to Europe and the West
Indies, ice to every major port, and bartering
furs from the northwest coast of America for
tea and silk and delicate porcelains in China.

When the British whaling industry fell off after 1820, the New Englanders, who had been whaling since colonial times, redoubled their efforts, penetrating, as Melville wrote in 1851, "even through Bering's Strait and into the remotest secret drawers and lockers of the world." Explorers penetrated even further, John Ross and Edward Parry into the Arctic in search of the northwest passage, and James Ross (the nephew) and Dumont d'Urville of France into the Antarctic.

Just when the steamship was about ready to make its mark in the world the sailing ship reached its peak of glory. The clipper, with its long narrow hull, knife-sharp bows, and huge display of canvas was designed for speed. It was developed in response to the demand for fresh tea from the Indies, and came into its own when the discovery of gold in America and Australia touched off a huge rush of immigrants to both countries. It seems to have been an American invention, and the first real clipper was certainly the *Rainbow* of 1845, designed by John Griffiths of New York. The fastest, and undoubtedly the finest sailing ship of all time, was Donald McKay's *Flying Cloud* of 1851, while his *Great Republic*, 325 feet long, was the largest wooden ship ever built. These magnificent ships, so briefly dominant, so beautiful, so efficient have captured the imagination (and quite rightly) of all those who love the sea. Their speed and maneuverability was prodigious. The fastest clippers could cross the Atlantic in 14 days and round Cape Horn from New York to San Francisco in 89 days (90,000 passengers were carried to California during the first year of the gold rush). Thanks to the training and discipline of the crews their masses of billowing sail could be raised and set as fast as those of any naval frigate; but of course the clippers could outsail any naval ship afloat. When the Civil War disrupted the trade of the American clippers, British clippers like the famous *Cutty Sark* took over until the inevitable development of the ocean-going steamer, as well as the opening of the Suez Canal in 1869 (which diverted the Eastern trade to steamers—for clippers could not negotiate the treacherous inland seas) eventually spelled the doom of the sailing ship. Huge four or five-masted, slow, iron-and-steel-hulled "Cape Horners"—built strictly for economy— survived into this century; but now even they have disappeared.

While the clippers were coursing the seas like nimble hares, the clumsy steamboats, like the tortoise of the fable, were inching slowly forward. On April 26, 1838, two steamers arrived in New York, inaugurating passenger service across the Atlantic. The little *Sirius*, loaded down with 94 passengers, had been built for the Irish Channel. She made the voyage entirely under steam, but burned up all her coal, her cabin doors and furniture, and even one mast. Four hours later the *Great Western*, built for the Great Western Railroad by that remarkable designer, Isambard Kingdom Brunel, steamed into New York with only eight passengers on board and plenty of coal left over. She was the first real transatlantic liner, and was followed by a number of other Great Western liners, including Brunel's handsome *Great Britain* of 1843, with a revolutionary iron hull and a screw propeller, which

105

106

107

85

108 *Five Japanese submarines, built by Americans for the Russo-Japanese War in 1905 and assembled in Japan by American technicians. They never saw action. Their design was that of U.S. Navy's first submarine fleet, the A-Class. Submarines were built for both sides during the war but none were used. Russo-Japanese War however saw extensive use of torpedoes, and in the Battle of Tsushima Straits the first large engagement between big gun warships.*

109

109   Prussian submarine, Wilhelm Bauer's "Brandtaucher," frightened
off Danish fleet blockading Kiel in 1850.
110   Ingenious "Turtle" of the American, David Bushnell, unsuccessfully
attacked British warships during the American War of Independence.

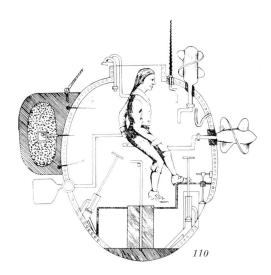

110

could carry 260 passengers and 1,200 tons of freight. After the *Great Western's* success, transatlantic steamship companies began to form—first the Cunard Line, opened by Samuel Cunard with the *Britannia's* first trip to Boston in 1840 (she was a wooden side-wheeler), then the Collins Line (U.S.A.) of 1849, the Hamburg-America Line of 1856, the Norddeutscher Lloyd of 1858, and the Compagnie Générale Transatlantique (the French Line) of 1864. About the same time American steamers began to cross the Pacific. In 1839 the Peninsula and Oriental Line began running ships to Alexandria to link with those of the East India Company coming up the Red Sea.

Passenger accommodations on these early steamers were far ahead of those found on the sailing ships. As far back as 1809 the *Clermont* had offered 54 "couchettes" for the night run to Albany, while the glittering splendors of the narrow interiors of the later Mississippi sternwheelers have seldom been surpassed. But the ocean liners had space to spare. French steamers of the 1840's could offer "all the desired amenities : commodious rooms, richly decorated salons furnished with taste and embellished with mirrors and rugs. . . ." But this was for the first class. Third class passengers, most of whom were emigrants, got "only a hammock, or a stay on the deck"; for around 1850 the emigrant trade, especially to the United States, began to grow by leaps and bounds. Lucky were those who could afford a steamer or a fast clipper ; most were still crowded into the noisome steerage of a slow sailing packet.

The most famous and least successful liner of the period was Brunel's gigantic *Great Eastern*, launched in 1858. She killed Brunel, ruined the line that built her, and as a passenger ship was a colossal failure, though she finally did good service laying ocean cables. She was 680 feet long, displaced 22,600 tons, and because of her size was launched sideways into the Thames. She was an iron ship, double hulled, equipped with both paddlewheels and a propeller. She could carry 4,000 passengers, but seldom did, for when she was put on the Atlantic run in 1860 she rolled horribly and was taken out of service two years later. Yet the *Great Eastern* was half a century ahead of her times. Her tonnage was not equalled until 1904.

Ocean steamers of a more ordinary variety made rapid progress during the second half of the nineteenth century. Hulls began to be built entirely of iron, and finally of steel. Though passengers felt "safer" with paddlewheels, the propeller eventually won acceptance. Sails disappeared even later. Size and speed increased with every new ship as two or more propellers and the triple-expansion engine became common. And in this period the specialized cargo ship began its career, starting out, after the opening of the Suez Canal, as a collier bringing coal to the various refueling ports, then beginning to take on other freight.

After 1850 Europe's mighty industrial revolution began to engulf the world. In half a century much of Asia and Africa was reduced to colonial status, while a massive flow of emigrants helped to build up the Americas as well as Australia and New Zealand. Western

111 The little "Elise," first steamboat to venture on to the ocean, is welcomed at Paris after a stormy, 17-hour voyage across the Channel from England and up the Seine River in 1816.
112 The "Friedrich Wilhelm," early river steamer on the Rhine. Note stagecoach on her deck.
113 A French river steamer which plied between Rouen and Le Havre on the Seine. Auxiliary sails were still considered necessary.
114 The "Great Western," first of the transatlantic steamers, leaves on her maiden voyage to New York in 1838. She was designed by Isambard K. Brunel.

113
114

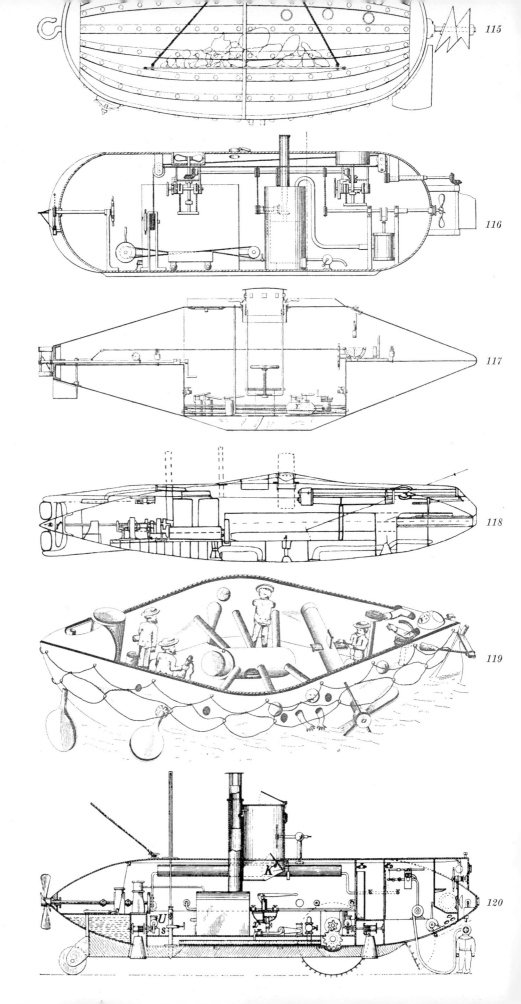

115

116

117

118

119

120

pressure even forced open the long-locked gates of Japan, after the American commodore, Matthew Calbraith Perry, had established commercial relations with Japan in 1854. And the immediate instrument of this expansion was the steamship—the packet, the liner, the warship. The naval establishments were the last to come to steam, because paddlewheels were considered too vulnerable for a combat ship. (Fulton's pioneer gunship, the *Demologos*, built for the American navy in 1814, had its paddle between double hulls.) Most navies started early with little steam frigates like the French *Sphinx* of 1829, but not until Francis Pettit Smith of England and John Ericsson of Sweden had invented a practical propeller (both in 1836) were men-of-war equipped with steam. Brunel's experimental *Rattler* of 1841 outpulled the paddle-steamer *Alecto* in a trial of strength in 1845. The French navy also tested the propeller, then in 1850 launched Dupuy de Lôme's man-of-war *Napoléon*, which was followed in 1852 by the British *Agamemnon* Both were still full rigged and wooden walled, with guns mounted broadside, but in both for the first time sail was auxiliary to steam. Somewhat earlier John Ericsson, who had gone to America, built the *Princeton* for the U.S. Navy.

After the advantages of steam warships and armored gun barges had been shown in the Crimean War of 1853-56, Dupuy de Lôme brought forth the first armored ship, *La Gloire* of 1859, plated with iron 10 to 12 centimeters thick. Alarmed, England launched its armored *Warrior* the next year. But it was the battle between the Confederate *Merrimac* and the Union *Monitor* in 1862, during the American

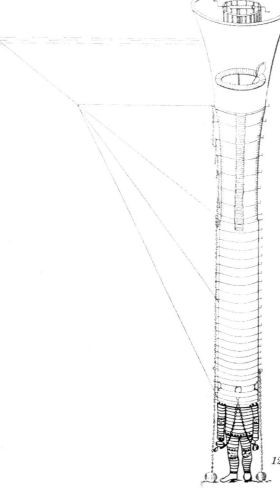

121

122 The "Great Eastern," designed by Brunel and launched in 1858, was half a century ahead of her times, yet she was a total failure, ending her days as a cable-laying ship. Her statistics are impressive. She was 680 ft. long, was made all of iron, and displaced 22,600 tons. She was equipped with both paddlewheels and a propeller (24 ft. in diameter), as well as six masts, and would make about 25 miles per hour. She could carry about 4,000 passengers (or 10,000 troops). But she never had enough passengers, and she killed Brunel.

Civil War, that advertised the ironclad to the world. The *Merrimac*, a converted frigate, was attacking the helpless Union fleet in Hampton Roads when John Ericsson's newly launched *Monitor* appeared, a raft-like little vessel with one of the first revolutionary gun turrets. The battle was as indecisive as it was famous, but it did lead to the use of armored gunboats during the rest of the war, particularly on the Mississippi during the Vicksburg campaign and in the battle of Mobile Bay. For the rest, the war was fought by wooden ships—steam or sail—the Union blockading the southern coastline and the Confederacy slipping its ships through the blockade and destroying Union shipping on the high seas with such redoutable steam raiders as the famous *Alabama*.

But the battleship race was on. The Spanish had launched their powerful armored *Numancia* in 1864, the Austrians an armored frigate in 1865. With the introduction of the explosive shell gun the broadside faded into history, leaving a few heavy guns mounted in *Monitor*-like turrets. Armor-plate grew thicker and sails disappeared, as in Britain's *Devastation* of 1873. The Battle of Lissa in 1866 introduced rams, which lasted for half a century. In 1876 the first big gun warships were launched in Italy under the naval genius, Benedetto Brin. The *Duilo* and the *Dandalo* boasted four huge 50-ton guns in two turrets. Britain's answer was the *Inflexible*, with 80-ton guns. By 1892, with Britain's *Royal Sovereign* class, the Big Ship had arrived. Steel-plated, with four principal guns, it also had an array of lighter guns and machine guns to use against the threat of the new torpedo boats. These small craft began to

be built in the 1870's, after Robert Whitehead's torpedo had been perfected.

The torpedo boat was much favored at this time, but its rival, the submarine, was still considered a "dangerous toy." After Fulton's abortive *Nautilus* there had been many attempts to perfect a submarine—the Prussian *Brandtaucher* of 1850, the French *Plongeur* of 1863, the Confederate *Hunley* of the American Civil War, which drowned four crews and went down with its only victim, a Union frigate. Not until the end of the century had technology advanced far enough to solve the complex problems of underwater navigation. Then in a burst of intense activity the basic principles were worked out by John P. Holland and Simon Lake in the United States, by Nordenfeldt in Sweden, Garrett in England, and Isaac Peral in Spain. France became a leader with its *Gymnote*, *Gustave Zédé*, and *Narval*, and its fleet of little electric *Goubets*. But John P. Holland's *Holland*, is generally recognized as the prototype of the modern submarine. Unlike the submarines of Lake and Nordenfeldt, which submerged straight down on an "even keel," the *Holland* was lighter than water, while its trimming tanks kept it in a nice adjustment of weight and balance. It was forced under water while in motion by its steering apparatus, diving like a porpoise. With its dual propulsion-gasoline motor on the surface, electric motor for submerged running—it was highly maneuverable. The submarine of World War II was a descendant of the *Holland*. The submarine today, powered by atomic energy and armed with a ballistic missile, threatens to become the battleship of the future.

123 Queen Victoria visits Napoleon III on board the "Bretagne" at Cherbourg in 1858. Men-of-war at this time had still not changed perceptibly from those of Nelson's day.

124-125 *The new and the old. Sailors reef the sails on a
French man-of-war in the 1840's. Behind : plans for
the White Star sister-ships, "Olympic" and "Titanic"
of 1912, among the first of the giant Atlantic luxury liners.*

While the wooden man-of-war ruled the seas unchallenged for over 200 years, the big gun battleship was able to maintain a shaky naval supremacy for less than 50 years. Its real enemy was the disruptive march of progress, for the first half of the twentieth century was a period of rapid change in maritime affairs as in everything else.

But for a time the battleship was the supreme expression of national strength on the seas, not only of the older naval powers of Europe but of new, rising powers—the United States, Japan, and Germany—whose naval victories first gave notice that the long held balance of power was about to be upset. Thus in 1898 the United States, with its fledgling fleet, easily crushed the seapower of Spain in the western waters, and in 1905 the Japanese, who had already revealed their growing naval strength in a brief war with China ten years before, checked Russia's ambitions in the East in a great sea battle in Tsushima Straits, one of the most devastating victories in history.

The Japanese ships at Tsushima were mostly British built, for Britain was still the acknowledged mistress of the seas. The very next year England's *Dreadnought*, with her huge 12-inch guns and 21-knot speed, made all other battleships obsolete and began the arms race that led to the First World War. Tonnage grew heavier, fuel oil replaced coal, the armored cruiser was developed, and smokeless powder and electric or hydraulic controls increased the rapidity of fire. And the big guns grew bigger, for artillery ruled the waves.

The arms race helped to bring on World War I, for by 1914, Germany, which had become

126

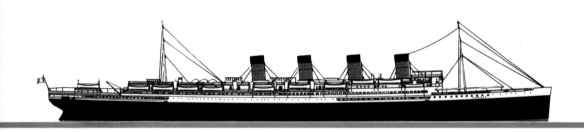

127

128

126 *"Mauretania", 1907, built for the Cunard Line. Length 790 feet, tonnage 31,938.*
127 *"France", 1912, built for the French Line. Length 720 feet, tonnage 23,666.*
128 *"Queen Elizabeth" 1939, built for the Cunard Line. Length 1.031 feet, tonnage 83,673.*
129 *"United States", 1952, built for the United States Line. Length 990 feet, tonnage 53,329.*
130 *"Christoforo Colombo" 1954, built for the Italian Line. Length 641 feet, tonnage 29,191.*
131 *"Rotterdam", 1960, built for the Holland-America Line. Length 748 feet, tonnage 38,645.*

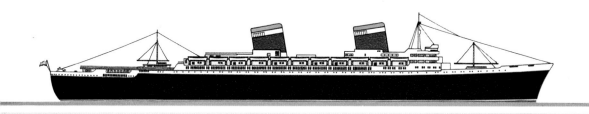

129

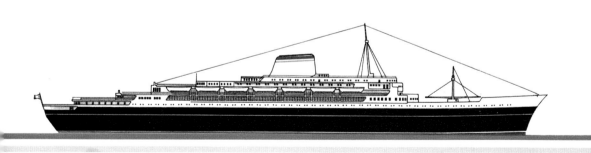

130

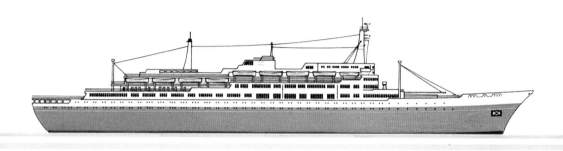

131

an active maritime power, had begun to threaten England with a high seas fleet second only to hers. During the first year of the war, moreover, when the armies had mired down on the western front, it became evident to many that the deadlock would have to be broken on the seas. The French and British fleets had fastened a naval blockade upon Germany which she would have to break, or lose any chance of victory. The Battle of Jutland in 1916, a head-on clash in the North Sea between the two most powerful fleets in the world, failed to loosen the British noose, although in the battle itself the British came off much the worst. A year earlier the British, in their turn, despairing of a breakthrough on the western front, had tried to turn Germany's flank by an amphibious attack upon the Dardanelles. Both operations failed, and the stalemate continued. How was Germany to break out of this encirclement ? The submarine was the obvious answer, for Britain's navy and sea communications were highly vulnerable to underseas attack.

The submarine, used by the Germans for the first time on the high seas, had already shown its power, sinking three British cruisers in 1914 with a large loss of life, and the great liner *Lusitania* in 1915, which helped to worsen relations with the United States. The German resort to the submarine was almost a success. By 1917 the Allies were losing over half a million tons of shipping a month. But by 1918, with the United States now in the war and building prefabricated "Liberty" ships on a mass basis, and with countermeasures such as the convoy system and depth charges, the tide began to turn.

During the last two years of the war the big surface ships had found little to do, for naval warfare had centered around the submarine. Nevertheless, in the postwar arms conferences, the big ships received most of the attention, tonnages being limited and further construction banned for ten years. while the submarines, carriers, and small ships, which were to dominate World War II, got away with much lighter penalties. A ratio of national tonnages, established at the Washington Conference of 1922, reflected the new balance of power—Britain and the United States first, Japan, second, and France and Italy third. By the opening of World War II the aircraft carrier, which had made its first appearance at the end of World War I, was well established in all the major navies, except for Italy and Germany. Ironically, Italy led the world in submarines in 1936, while France and Japan were building huge "cruiser" submersibles (like France's 2,800-ton *Surcouf*) which were to have little or no effect upon World War II.

There were other surprises in the Second World War. The battleship was finally dethroned, the carrier taking its place at the head of the fleet. At the beginning of the war the British lost *Royal Oak* to a submarine, and later the *Prince of Wales* and *Repulse* to Japanese planes in the Pacific. The Germans had built some fine, modern ships—the *Graf Spee*, *Bismarck*, *Scharnhorst*, *Gneisenau*, and *Prinz Eugen*—but after some deadly forays against Allied shipping they were all hunted down or immobilized by 1942. The French never had a chance to use their renascent fleet. Part of it was reluctantly destroyed by the British at

132 *Life preserver of the 1840's.*

Oran in 1940 and most of the rest scuttled at Toulon in 1942 to keep it from the Germans. The Italian fleet, without carrier protection, was defeated by the British at Cape Matapan in 1941 and was thereafter ignominiously kept in port for lack of fuel. The Japanese aircraft almost destroyed the American Pacific fleet at Pearl Harbor in 1941, while the bulk of the Japanese fleet, including such monsters as the 45,000-ton *Yamato*, was sent to the bottom in the American counteroffensive of 1945.

In the Atlantic, submarine warfare was relatively less effective than it was during World War I, though at the height of the battle the Germans often had 400 submarines at sea at once. Antisubmarine measures, on the other hand, were even more effective, and by 1943 had substantially overcome the menace. In the Pacific, however, American submarines played a really decisive role in the defeat of Japan, accounting for over half of the merchant ships sunk and nearly 30 per cent of Japanese naval units. In the Pacific the carrier, too, came into its own, fighting such great aero-naval battles as those of the Coral Sea and Midway and later, grouped in task forces with other naval ships, carrying the war up the ladder of islands to Japan. By 1945, there were 150 carriers, British and American, operating in the Pacific.

World War II also saw the development of highly organized amphibious assaults, beginning with Germany's invasion of Norway in 1940 and perhaps including the extraordinary amphibious withdrawal, under German fire, of the British army from Dunkerque in the same year. A variety of specialized landing craft were developed for the massive Allied landings in North Africa, Sicily, Normandy, and Southern France. The Normandy invasion, which was supported by over 10,000 planes, 80 warships, and 4,000 other ships, saw partially successful attempts to install artificial harbors on the French coast. Similar landing techniques were employed in the Pacific for the capture of island after island and for the larger landings such as that on Leyte in the Philippines.

Ocean liners, used as troopships, also played their part in the war. By carrying, between them, a million and a half soldiers overseas, the giant *Queen Mary* and *Queen Elizabeth*, it has been estimated, may have shortened the war by as much as a year. This statistic alone indicates how far the ocean liner had come since the *Great Western* of 1838, with its 1,755 tons and 8-knot speed. By contrast, the *Queen Elizabeth* steams at 30 knots and displaces 83,673 tons. The era of the giant Atlantic liners—veritable floating hotels, which competed with each other in terms of speed, size, passenger comfort, and national prestige—opened with the *Mauretania* of 1907 (and her ill-fated sister-ship, the *Lusitania*). The *Mauretania*, with her clean lines, four imposing funnels, and great speed (she was pushed at 25 knots by four propellers) held the Atlantic blue ribbon for over 22 years, making the trip in about four days, 16 hours, which is a respectable time even for today. She and her sister were the first large liners with turbine drive (though among the last to be hand fired with coal instead of oil, requiring 324 firemen and trimmers to shovel about 1,000 tons of coal into her boilers per day!). In the era of the

133

*133 View aft on the new giant
French liner, "France."
Despite stiff competition from
airlines, new Atlantic liners,
emphasizing speed and luxury,
are still being built. Era of
the big liners began with the
"Mauretania" of 1907,
culminated before World War II
with* **Britain's** *"Queen
Elizabeth" and "Queen Mary"
and France's "Normandie."
134 Japanese freighter unloading.
Japanese shipbuilding now leads
the world. Since World War II
the world's merchant fleet has
increased by leaps and bounds,
both in quantity and in tonnage.*

134

*135 Many nations, large and small, now have
active fishing fleets. Fishing techniques have been
revolutionized. Whalers are now floating factories
as large as tankers and process tons of oil.*

great Atlantic liners everybody had favorites :
The *Olympic* of 1912 (the *Titanic*, which hit
an iceberg and sank on her maiden voyage, was
her sister-ship), the wonderful *Aquitania* of
1914, retired in 1950, the faithful *Ile-de-France*
of 1927, the German *Bremen* of 1929, Italy's
Rex of 1933, the richly decorated *Normandie*
of 1935 (burned at her dock in New York in
1942), the Dutch *Nieuw Amsterdam* of 1938.
These were magnificent ships whose individual personalities endeared them to millions.

Despite enormous destruction in two global
wars, the world's merchant fleet has steadily
grown larger and more specialized. Some mixed
ships carry passengers and cargo ; many
freighters are equipped with refrigerating
systems, while the fruit carriers, "banana
boats," must maintain an even interior tem-
perature to preserve their perishable cargo. The
most spectacular development has been in the
oil-carrying tankers. Starting in 1886 with a
few little ships of under 3,000 tons, the tanker
fleet by the eve of World War II had grown to
16 per cent of the world's shipping and today,
especially under the ownership of enterprising
Greek merchant-princes, has been constantly
enlarged, with tankers of 30,000 and even up
to 100,000 tons in regular service. As with the
Atlantic queens, speed and tonnage have
become an economic necessity. France's *Esso
Parentis* of 1958, for instance, a 38,000-ton
mammoth, can make over 17 knots. And more
and more of the merchant fleet—and liners
too—have turned to Diesel power, threatening
to end the reign of steam less than a hundred
years after its first triumphs. The most specialized of commercial ships, the fishing boats, have

become mechanized floating factories—especially the whalers—capable of catching and
processing incredible tonnages of fish.

There are very few commercial sailing craft
left. But the sailing yacht today enjoys a greater
popularity than ever before. Pleasure boats
have been known since earliest times, but it
was Charles II of England, himself enamored
of the sea, who introduced the sailing yacht
to the world. The Dutch *jacht* was a small,
swift sailing craft, lightly armed, often used
for state business such as transporting important people. Charles II built 26 yachts, and used
them not only for his royal business but also
for pleasure and for racing. In the eighteenth
century, when naval warfare had become an
art of maneuvering under sail, yachting by
reflection began to grow in popularity. The
Cowes regattas started in 1810, and by mid-
century yachting had spread to many countries,
and such great international regattas as the
America's Cup had become regular events. So
diverse were the types of yachts in competition,
however, that the "handicap" was adopted in
1878, and in 1907, with the founding of the
International Yacht Racing Union, uniform
regulations for regattas and classes of boats
were laid down. The steam yacht appeared as
early as 1825, (though it was frowned upon in
yachting circles until the second half of the
century) and soon became a necessity in royal
establishments as well as in those of million-
aires like the Astors and Vanderbilts of the
United States. The motorboat, the "poor man's
yacht," had its origin around the turn of the
century in the fragile racing "autoboats,"
powered with automobile engines. In the 1920's

136

it began to be taken up by the great middle class. Today, even the graceful sailing yacht, once the exclusive property of the rich, can become the cherished possession of anybody with a little extra cash and a love of the sea.

Since World War II the navies of the world have been in rapid transition, and the future is still not clear. Britain, once ruler of the seas, is now in third place behind Russia and the United States, with the latter leading all others by a wide margin. Since conventional artillery has lost its importance, the battleship has given way to the carrier. Cruisers, destroyers, and lesser craft now dance attendance upon the carrier as they once did upon the battleship. The carrier's weapon is the airplane, usually with nuclear bombing capability, as on the United States' growing fleet of supercarriers of the *Forrestal* type (60,000 tons), which can launch 32 heavy planes in four minutes. The carrier's function is to act as a mobile base, available for operations in any part of the world. The weapon of the cruiser and other surface craft is the guided missile, capable of antiaircraft defense, of ship-to-ship and ship-to-shore bombardment. To increase the range and mobility of its surface warships the United States has embarked upon a program of atomic-powered vessels, such as the giant, 85,350-ton carrier *Enterprise*, and the guided missile cruiser, *Long Beach*. The *Enterprise*, the largest military ship in the world, can handle up to 100 aircraft and develops more than 200,000 horse-power from her eight reactors.

In a day when the major nations depend upon atom bomb-carrying intercontinental missiles and strategic bombers for their primary defense, the role of the surface fleet is a controversial matter. Its greatest usefulness may be in dealing with smaller wars, where mobility is of prime importance, and certainly in antisubmarine warfare; for that once-despised arm of the fleet, the submarine, has taken on a new and frightening importance. The Russians, with no carrier force, boast the largest submarine force in the world, including a number of nuclear-powered craft. The United States leads, however, in the area of nuclear-powered submarines, with a growing fleet of fast, fish-shaped monsters capable of operating submerged for months at a time and delivering on enemy targets, from beneath the water, up to 16 Polaris ballistic missiles with a range of well over 1,000 miles. The submarine *Nautilus*, the world's first atomic-powered vessel, launched in 1954, was the creation of hard-driving Admiral Hyman G. Rickover of the U.S. Navy, who pushed the project through against almost insuperable odds and in record time. Since then the United States has launched a large fleet of atomic submarines of various types, including the mammoth radar picket *Triton*, with two reactors, which is a veritable floating electronics laboratory. The atomic submarine, with its enormous potential, may well become the battleship of the future—and perhaps the passenger and commercial ship of the future as well.

Both on the surface of the water and beneath it the future is a surmise. Atomic power has been applied to non-military surface ships, notably the American merchant ship *Savannah* and the Russian icebreaker *Lenin*, though it

136 The "islands" of the "Enterprise," the United States' newest and largest carrier and first with nuclear power. Diagonal bars on the upper part of the island are part of the ship's complex radar system. The "Enterprise" is 1,123 ft. long, displaces 85,350 tons, is powered by eight reactors.
137 The "Enterprise" during trials. Her four steam catapults can launch her planes—up to 100—at a rate of one every 15 seconds. She carries a crew of 4,600 sailors and airmen.

137

*138 The nuclear-powered
"George Washington" of the
U.S. Navy is armed with
16 Polaris missiles which
can be fired from beneath the
water. Each missile, nuclear-
tipped, will travel well over
1,000 miles. The atomic
submarine, with the giant
nuclear-powered carrier, has now
become a leading naval strategic
weapon. The U.S. Navy is
planning to built at least 50
Polaris submarines armed with a
total of 800 missiles. The nuclear
submarine, now a weapon,
may in time develop into
the ship of tomorrow.*

is not yet competitive in price with conventionally powered ships. In the meantime, with air travel across the Atlantic increasing fourfold in the last decade, while sea travel has begun to decline, the future of the great Atlantic liner is in doubt, France has taken a bold gamble with her magnificent new *France* (1962), and the Italian Line is putting two new large ships into service in 1964 ; but England's Cunard Line has recently decided not to go ahead with a replacement for the aging *Queen Mary*. The future undoubtedly lies with the smaller, more versatile ocean liner which can take advantage both of regular passenger demands and of the growing popularity of ocean cruises. Experiments with new types of boats may hint at an even more distant future. The "hovercraft," which rides on a cushion of air, may soon be used for a cross-Channel ferry, while hydrofoil craft, whose wing foils lift the boat's hull above the waves to allow for greater speed, are already providing rapid commuting service in many parts of the world. In underwater research, the "bathyscaph" of Professor Auguste Piccard and his son Jacques, a diving vessel, reached a record depth of 37,000 feet in the Pacific in 1960 in a research program that takes on new importance with the advent of the atomic submarine.

But whether on the surface of the ocean or under it, skimming like seagulls on swift hydrofoils, breathing the salt wind from the deck of a liner, moving submerged and silent in the shadowed depths, watching the spank of a white sail on a windy day, or just pulling the creaking oar of a rowboat, men will never cease to go down to the sea.

139　"They that go down to the sea in ships. . . ."

Noah's Ark, medieval woodcut

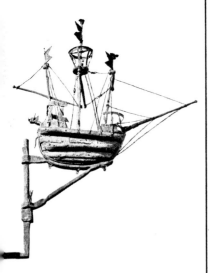

chronology

B.C.

4000 The sailboat may have first appeared in Mesopotamia.

2000 Pharaoh Senusret cuts boat canal from the Nile to the Red Sea.

1500 Queen Hatshepsut of Egypt sends a state-organized expedition to Punt.

1190 Ramses III of Egypt turns back an invasion by the piratical Sea Peoples at naval battle fought off the coast of Egypt.

1184 Traditional date for the fall of Troy.

814 Founding of Carthage in North Africa by colonists from Phoenician Tyre.

600 Phoenician sailors, serving Pharaoh Necho of Egypt, may have circumnavigated Africa from east to west.

550 The Carthaginian general, Hanno, leads an expedition down the west coast of Africa.

480 The Greeks defeat the fleet of Xerxes at Salamis, off Athens.

330 Pytheas, a Greek explorer from Marseilles, leads an expedition north to England and into the North Sea.

Portugese globe, 16th Century

264 Beginning of the First Punic War, Rome against Carthage, and rise of Roman seapower.

146 Destruction of Carthage and Corinth at the end of the Third Punic War, leaving Rome in control of the waters of the western Mediterranean.

67 Pompey the Great drives the Cicilian pirates, out of the Mediterranean.

31 Battle of Actium, establishes Roman naval domination of the Mediterranean.

A.D.

150 Greek astronomer-geographer Claudius Ptolemy publishes his geography, influential during the Middle Ages.

673- Moslem fleet driven from
678 Constantinople by Greek fire.

762 Foundation of Baghdad on the Tigris, which became a great commercial center for shipping and trade.

Ancient lighthouse

844 Vikings explore the western coast of Spain. In succeeding years they discover Iceland, Labrador, and Greenland.

1000 Leif Ericsson discovers the North American coast.

1066 William the Conqueror of Normandy invades England with a fleet of long boats, defeats Harold, seizes the throne.

1098 The First Crusade opens, largely a land operation.

1270 The Eighth Crusade, last important crusade, with ships furnished by Venice and Genoa.

1294 Creation of the « Clos des Galées », at Rouen, the first French shipyard.

1340 Battle of Sluys. Edward III of England defeats the French fleet early in the Hundred Years' War, and establishes English naval supremacy in the Channel.

Japanese merchant junk

Barbarossa

Jean Bart

1372 French and Castilian fleets regain control of the Channel at the Battle of La Rochelle.

1418 Prince Henry (The Navigator) of Portugal, having founded an academy at Sagres to study navigation and cosmography, begins to send out ships on voyages of exploration.

1460 Portuguese explorers of Africa reach what is now Sierra Leone.

1492 Colombus's first voyage for Spain. He reaches the Bahamas in the New World.

1493 Pope Alexander VI establishes a demarcation line from pole to pole through the Atlantic, dividing Spanish and Portuguese areas of exploration and settlement.

1497- Vasco de Gama of Portugal
1498 rounds Africa and reaches India.

1497- John Cabot explores
1498 Labrador, Nova Scotia, and Newfoundland for England.

1500 Pedro Cabral and a Portuguese fleet lay claim to Brazil, then sail back to India to open trade.

1519- A Spanish expedition, under
1522 Ferdinand Magellan, circumnavigates the globe.

1524 Giovanni da Verrazzano of Florence explores the coastline of North America for France.

1535- Jacques Cartier explores
1541 the Saint Lawrence River for France.

1542 Portuguese ships first visit Japan.

1553- Sir Hugh Willoughby and
1554 Richard Chancellor of England sail to the north coast of Russia.

1571 Naval battle of Lepanto, in which Christian forces of the Holy League defeat a Turkish fleet in the last major clash between war galleys.

1572- Francis Drake of England
1580 sails around the world.

1576 Sir Martin Frobisher attempts to find a northwest passage, reaches Baffin Land.

1583 Sir Humphrey Gilbert claims Newfoundland for the English.

1585 John Davis, searching for a northwest passage, reaches Davis Straits.

1588 The Spanish Armada is defeated by the English fleet in the Channel.

1594- Willem Barents of Holland,
1597 seeking a northeast passage, explores Novaya Zemlya and Spitzbergen.

1600 Founding of the British East India Company.

1602 Founding of the Dutch East India Company.

1662- Jean-Baptiste Colbert in
1683 power in France. He builds up the French navy, stimulates interest in the merchant marine and trading companies.

1679- La Salle explores the
1689 Great Lakes and Mississippi regions of North America for France.

1695 Denis Papin invents his "cooking pot" steam engine.

1707 Denis Papin tests a paddlewheel boat.

1763 William Henry experiments with a steamboat.

1767- Bougainville explores the
1769 Pacific, discovering several islands.

1768- Captain James Cook makes
1779 three voyages of exploration in the Pacific.

1772 Scottish inventor James Watt creates the modern steam engine.

Andrea Doria

Early paddlewheel boat

Early diver's costume

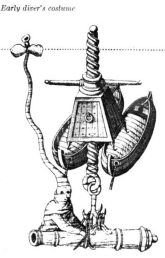

Jacques Cartier

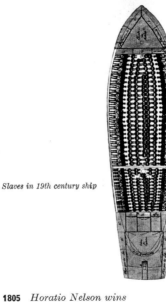

The Jolly Roger

Slaves in 19th century ship

1774 The steamboat built by the Counts of Auxiron and Follenay is sunk.

1775 David Bushnell's "Turtle" submarine unsuccessfully attacks British ships.

1780 Patrick Miller tests a series of two- and three-hulled paddlewheel boats.

1780-1798 John Fitch experiments with a series of steamboats.

1783 Count Jouffroy d'Abban's steamboat is tested on the Seine.

1797 Robert Fulton presents the French with a project for a submarine, the " Nautilus ".

1798 Nelson destroys the French, fleet in the harbor of Abukir.

1802 American inventor Oliver Evans tests his amphibious steam dredge " Orukter Amphibolos" on land and water.

1802 The steam tugboat "Charlotte Dundas," driven by a Symington engine, is successfully tested in Scotland.

1803 Robert Fulton, in association with Robert Livingston, builds a steamboat in Paris, tests it on the Seine.

1805 Horatio Nelson wins the Battle of Trafalgar.

1807 Robert Fulton's "Clermont" makes her first trips on the Hudson River between New York and Albany.

1808 John Steven's "Phoenix" is the first steamboat to make an ocean voyage.

1812 The first steamboat appears on the Mississippi river.

1812 Henry Bell's "Comet," a paddlewheel steamboat, goes into service on the Clyde.

1816 The little steamer "Elise" crosses the Channel.

1818 Captain John Ross and Lieutenant Edward Parry make an exploration of Baffin Bay.

1819 The first crossing of the Atlantic by steamboat is made by the "Savannah" which crosses from the United States to England, traveling partly under steam.

1827 Destruction of the Egyptian fleet by British, French, and Russian squadrons in the Battle of Navarino.

1829 Launching of the first French steam warship, the paddlewheel "Sphinx ".

1831 In the course of an arctic exploration with his uncle John Ross, James Clark Ross locates the north magnetic pole.

1832 Frenchman Frederick Sauvage patents a propeller.

1834 The little propeller-driven American steamer "Midas" sails from New York to China.

1836 Englishman Francis Pettit Smith and Swedish engineer John Ericsson both take out patents on screw propellers.

1838 The steamship "Sirius" is the first to cross the Atlantic completely under steam, arriving in New York four hours before the "Great Western".

1840 With the inaugural voyage of the steamer "Britannia" the Cunard Line begins the first regular service between Europe and North America.

1843 Isambard K. Brunel's "Great Britain" is launched.

1845 The "Rainbow," the first of the clippers, is launched in New York.

1850 Wilhelm Bauer's submarine "Brandtaucher" is tested at Kiel.

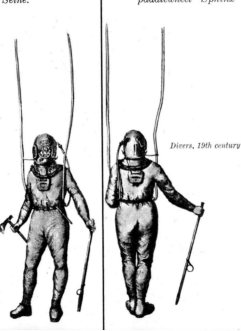

Divers, 19th century

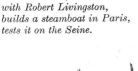

Balsa boat, used in surf

Fishing hook, 18th century

Holland's first submarine

1851 Donald McKay's "Flying Cloud," considered to be the fastest of American clippers, is launched.

1853 Largest of the clippers, McKay's "Great Republic" is also the biggest wooden vessel ever built.

1853-1856 The Crimean War shows up the advantages of steam warships and armored gun barges.

1858 Brunel's gigantic passenger steamer "Great Eastern" is launched.

1858 France launches the first armored ship, Dupuy de Lôme's "La Gloire".

1860 England launches her first armored ship, the frigate "Warrior."

1862 In the first engagement between iron-clad vessels, the Confederate "Merrimac" and the Union "Monitor" fight at Hampton Roads.

1863 The submarine "Le Plongeur," driven by compressed air, is built in France by Bourgois and Brun.

1866 Robert Whitehead invents the first efficient torpedo, a weapon that is to change naval warfare.

1869 Opening of the Suez Canal, engineered by Frenchman Ferdinand de Lesseps, which cut the distance between London and Bombay nearly in half.

1876 Designer Benedetto Brin builds the "Duilio" and the "Dandalo", big-gun battleships, for the Italian navy.

1878 John P. Holland builds his first submarine, "Boat No. 1."

1880 Thorsten Nordenfeldt, a Swede, experiments with submarines armed with the Whitehead torpedo.

1885 First of Goubet's little electric submarines built.

1888 Frenchman Gustave Zédé builds the submarine "Gymnote."

1888 Isaac Peral builds an amazing submarine for the Spanish navy.

1892 Britain builds seven new ships of the "Royal Sovereign" class.

1893 France constructs the "Charles Martel," monster battleship typical of the French "floating fortresses" of the period.

English steamer at Canton, 1840

John P. Holland, inventor

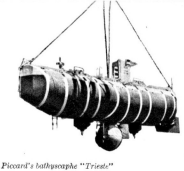

Piccard's bathyscaphe "Trieste"

Squid found on Arctic voyage

How to splice a rope

1893 The French submarine "Gustave Zédé" is launched and is a success.

1897 John P. Holland's submarine the "Holland" is launched.

1897 Simon Lake, life-long competitor of Holland, launches his submarine the "Argonaut."

1898 The United States fleet crushes the Spanish in the Spanish-American War.

1899 Launching of Laubeuf's submarine "Narval," which served the French navy until 1908.

1903-1906 Captain Roald Amundsen navigates the northwest passage.

1905 The Russian fleet is destroyed by the Japanese at the Battle of Tsushima straits.

1906 Launching of Britain's "Dreadnought."

1907 Launching of the Cunard Line's "Mauretania," holder of the Atlantic blue ribbon for over 22 years.

1912 White Star Liner "Titanic" sunk by an iceberg in North Atlantic.

1914 Opening of the Panama Canal.

1915 Allied attempts to break through the Dardanelles fail.

1915 The Germans begin a submarine blockade of Great Britain, their submarines sinking a number of ships, including the passenger ship "Lusitania."

1916 At the Battle of Jutland the German and British fleets fight in the North Sea.

1917 Commissioning of HMS "Furious," first aircraft carrier.

1922 The Washington Conference sees the signing of a naval armaments treaty.

1922 Commissioning of the first United States aircraft carrier, "Langley."

1941 The British dreadnought "Hood" is sunk by the giant German battleship "Bismark," sunk in turn three days later by British air and naval forces.

1941 The Japanese attack the American bases at Pearl Harbor and on the Philippines and British forces in Hongkong and Malaya.

1942 Battles of the Coral Sea and of Midway, which proved the importance of the aircraft carrier.

1942 American and British forces make an amphibious invasion of French North Africa.

1942 The main part of the French fleet is scuttled by its crews in Toulon to keep it out of German hands.

1943 Allied forces invade Sicily in a mass amphibious attack. Later in the year the Allies land in southern Italy, in another amphibious invasion.

1944 Allied D-Day invasion of Normandy, June 6.

1944 American invasion troops take island after island from the Japanese in the Pacific,

1954 Launching of the American submarine "Nautilus," first nuclear-powered ship.

1958 The "Nautilus" and the nuclear submarine "Skate" cross from the Atlantic to the Pacific under the polar ice.

1959 Launching of the nuclear merchant ship "Savannah."

1960 The nuclear aircraft carrier "Enterprise," the biggest warship in the world, is launched.

1960 The French line launches its huge passenger liner "France."

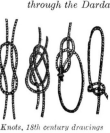

Knots, 18th century drawings

Ship in a bottle

Tattoo designs

*Amony those who have assisted
in the preparation of this book
grateful acknowledgement must
be made to the following members
of the ENI staff :
Penny Muller, Eric Tschumi,
Nicolas Bouvier, as well as
to Charles Dollfus and the
Musée de la Marine, both of Paris*

credits